Engaging Revelation

Engaging Revelation

Mark Braaten

WIPF & STOCK · Eugene, Oregon

ENGAGING REVELATION

Copyright © 2024 Mark Braaten. All rights reserved. Except for brief quotations in critical publications or reviews, no part of this book may be reproduced in any manner without prior written permission from the publisher. Write: Permissions, Wipf and Stock Publishers, 199 W. 8th Ave., Suite 3, Eugene, OR 97401.

Wipf & Stock
An Imprint of Wipf and Stock Publishers
199 W. 8th Ave., Suite 3
Eugene, OR 97401

www.wipfandstock.com

PAPERBACK ISBN: 979-8-3852-2657-3
HARDCOVER ISBN: 979-8-3852-2658-0
EBOOK ISBN: 979-8-3852-2659-7

VERSION NUMBER 09/03/24

Scripture quotations are from the New Revised Standard Version Bible, copyright 1989, Division of Christian Education of the National Council of the Churches of Christ in the United States of America. Used by Permission. All rights reserved.

To Karen—
Whose love and support has given me the richness of life.

To Amber and Christopher and Cassaundra,
and Luke and Rachel—
What a joy to see your lives unfold!

To Skylar and Scarlett and Sophia—
What gifts of promise and grace!

Contents

Preface | ix
Introduction: Promise and Warning | xi

Section 1: A Book of Promise | 1
Section 2: The Risen Jesus | 5
Section 3: The Congregation in Ephesus: A Less Than Loving Faith | 11
Section 4: The Congregation in Pergamum: Called to Be Distinctively Different | 16
Section 5: The Congregation in Laodicea: A Lukewarm Faith | 23
Section 6: There Is a Throne | 27
Section 7: The Lion and the Lamb: Or Better—the Lion Is the Lamb! | 33
Section 8: The Four Horsemen | 39
Section 9: Sealed in Christ: Who Can Stand? Those Who Are Sealed in Jesus! | 45
Section 10: Faithful Witnessing | 49
Section 11: Judgment in Revelation | 55
Section 12: Rapture or Not! | 63
Section 13: 666 | 70
Section 14: Pick a Side | 76

Contents

Section 15: Come Out of Her! Revelation 18 for
            Yesterday, Today, and Tomorrow | 81
Section 16: Armageddon | 86
Section 17: The Supper of the Birds | 92
Section 18: The Millennium | 98
Section 19: The Great White Throne | 104
Section 20: The New Jerusalem—Part 1 | 109
Section 21: The New Jerusalem—Part 2 | 114

Bibliography | 119

Preface

THERE IS A STORY of a sixty-four-year-old pastor who gave a particularly good sermon one Sunday morning. After worship one of the parishioners talked with the pastor and asked, "How long did you work on that sermon?" The pastor replied, "Sixty-four years." His answer shared that the sermon was a result of all that he had learned in his lifetime.

I believe I've been working on this book for thirty years. About thirty years ago I started a study of Revelation. I was determined to understand this last book of the Bible, so I started a journey that has turned into a life-long adventure. For thirty-plus years I've been studying, praying, reflecting, taking classes, working on degrees, teaching, and conversing on Revelation. This book is a pulling together of those thirty years of work. It has been a joyful journey, and I hope I can share with you some of the joy of it. I pray that our Lord blesses you and reveals Himself to you as you reflect on his gift of Revelation.

I have to say some thank yous. First and foremost, thank you to my wife, Karen. It is your support and love and encouragement that has made these adventures of mine possible. I couldn't have done all the studying and reflecting and teaching without your support and strength. You have enriched my life and the lives of so many others. Thank you for being my partner in all of this.

Thank you to our children, Amber and Christopher and Cassaundra, and our daughter- and son-in-law, Rachel and Luke.

Preface

You have gifted my life and in your own ways have shown me the wonder of grace.

I have to mention our new grandchildren, Skylar, Scarlett, and Sophia. You have helped me to appreciate anew the whole reality of promise.

Finally, to the readers of this book, may our Lord bless you as you engage with the wonder of the book of Revelation.

Introduction
Promise and Warning

REVELATION IS A BOOK of promise and warning. Both are powerfully proclaimed, both are essential for understanding the book. We have to carefully take stock of both as we seek to understand this magnificent last book of the Bible.

Revelation certainly is a book with strong words of warning and judgment. You don't have to read far into the book to feel stunned by many of the images. Some of the most graphic scenes of judgment in the Bible are found in the pages of this book. To list only a few, in the pages of Revelation we will encounter Death and Hades being given authority over a quarter of the earth (6:7–8), the sun turning black and stars falling to the earth (6:12–13), grotesque locust-like creatures ravaging and attacking people (9:1–11), horrifying hordes of mounted cavalry with horses spewing smoke and sulfur that kill scores of people (9:13–19), and a burning and smoldering lake of fire for Satan and his cohorts (19:20 and 20:10). We will have to take a good look at these images and ask carefully about their message for us.

We also need to quickly add, Revelation is a book of promise. Promise! Rich, magnificent, life transforming promises! Some of the most poignant, life-giving words of hope in the entire Bible are found in Revelation. We will encounter amazing images of having our tears dried by God's own hand (7:17), of experiencing the glory of the new heaven and the new earth (chs. 21 and 22), of dwelling in the sheltering presence of our Creator (7:15), of having the totality of our sins washed away by the blood of Jesus (7:14), of eternal rejoicing in the victory of our Savior (19:6–8). There are so many images of hope and newness that just cascade over us! Revelation is a beautiful invitation to come to the crucified yet risen Lord who gives new life to us and to the world!

Revelation is a book of promise and warning. To appreciate Revelation, we need to hear both. In fact, as we dive into the book, we will discover that the warnings and promises work together to drive us to the true center of the book, our Savior Jesus Christ.

Just a note as to how we will proceed. We are going to start with promise. So much of modern writing on Revelation focuses almost exclusively on the words of judgment; we are going to counteract that and start with promise. We will then work our way through the book of Revelation, looking at the images and messages of the book, with its rich intertwining of promise and warning. In section 11 we will focus particularly on how judgment and warning function in Revelation. Throughout our journey we will look at the richness and power of this last book of the Bible. The intent is to let the book of Revelation speak for itself, with all its force and wonder. As we listen and explore, we will be led to the one who is Lord and Savior, Alpha and Omega, Jesus Christ!

Section 1

A Book of Promise

REVELATION OVERFLOWS WITH PROMISES—RICH, magnificent, life transforming and world transforming promises! One of my fears is that in many of our modern interpretations of Revelation we get so caught up in the images of warning and judgment that we overlook the promises. Now to be sure, we will deal with the images of warning and judgment as we read our way through Revelation. But let's start with listening to the incredible promises that also fill this book. Revelation is ultimately a message of hope for a world in pain. It is God's promise that not only is his future the ultimate future for all reality but that future is even now breaking into our present.

Revelation contains some of the most powerful promises in the Bible. They are promises to build life on, promises to sustain the people of God in all that comes. A fun and helpful exercise in Revelation is to read through the book and note all the promises. Underline them if you would like; make notes on a piece of paper. Look for the promises. You will be amazed at all that God is about.

Let me highlight some of the promises for you:

First, in Rev 1:17-18, Jesus said, "Do not be afraid; I am the first and the last, and the living one. I was dead, and see, I am alive forever and ever; and I have the keys of Death and of Hades." Jesus promises us, commands us, that we don't need to live in fear. We belong to Him and He has conquered all that can befall us. In the midst of a world of despair and loss, Jesus has us in the palm of his hand. Jesus died, but He rose from the dead. Now as the risen one, He tells us that nothing, not even death, will stop his care for us. Even when we face our inevitable deaths, Jesus reminds us that He has the keys of death and Hades!

Second, in Rev 7:15–17, John writes,

> For this reason they [namely us, the people of God!] are before the throne of God,
> and worship him day and night within his temple;
> and the one who is seated on the throne will shelter them.
> They [namely us!] will hunger no more, and thirst no more;
> the sun will not strike them,
> nor any scorching heat;
> for the Lamb at the center of the throne will be their shepherd,
> and he will guide them to springs of the water of life,
> and God will wipe away every tear from their eyes.

There are enough promises here for three or four sermons! We, the humble people of God, will be before the very throne of God. In joy we will serve Him and be sheltered by Him. No longer will we be afflicted by hunger or thirst or scorching heat. For Jesus will be our shepherd and guide us to living water. What a view of what God has in store for us! Then Revelation goes even further—God will wipe away every tear from our eyes. I especially love this last promise. I envision a baby in the night who cries out in fear. All parents have had that happen, and we know what to do when that happens. We quickly go to the baby, pick the baby up, cuddle the baby, wipe away the tears, and assure the child that things are alright. That, the Bible is saying, is what God does for us. God, as a loving parent, will be there for us. In fact He picks us up and cares for us. God Himself will gently and tenderly wipe away our tears. What a picture of our heavenly Father!

Third, in Rev 21:3–4, John writes,

> See, the home of God is among mortals.
> He will dwell with them;

> they will be his peoples,
> and God himself will be with them;
> he will wipe every tear from their eyes.
> Death will be no more;
> mourning and crying and pain will be no more,
> for the first things have passed away.

The promises just keep coming; they literally cascade over themselves. God promises to dwell with us and we will be his people. God isn't some distant reality, far removed from his creation. He is, rather, in our very midst. As God has revealed in Jesus who is Emmanuel (God with us!), God's will is to be in the midst of his people. God promises to do just that.

Then it gets even better. The reading proclaims that we are the people of God. Think about that for a minute. God has promised to be God for us! In other words, we belong to the Almighty, and that means there is a dignity and specialness to each of our lives. We aren't just happenstances of an uncaring universe; rather we are lovingly and purposefully created by the loving Father. We are claimed by the Lord of creation, redeemed and cared for by Him! That means we are people of identity and worth and value. That is the promise given in our baptisms, and it is the promise for all of this life and the new life to come. That is the deepest reality of who we are! We are the people of the eternal One. The God of the cosmos, He is God for you and me.

The promises still keep coming. God again reminds us that He will wipe away our tears. Death and mourning and crying and pain will be wiped away. God's victory for us is complete. Nothing can stop the grace of our God.

Fourth, in Rev 21:5, John writes, "And the one who was seated on the throne said, 'See, I am making all things new.'" This is my favorite promise in Revelation. God is making all things new: you, me, our congregations, this world. All things are being made new. Sin and death have wreaked havoc on this creation. We ache in the pains of this old world. But there is a new world a-coming; there is a new world breaking in even now! New life and transformation and hope are happening in this old creation, for God is making this world new.

I like to note what God doesn't say here. God doesn't say, "I will make all new things." God could have said that. In fact, it would have been easier for Him to do that. God could have looked at our lives and this world and said, it is hopeless. God could have just wiped it all out and started over. God doesn't do that. His love for us is too great. God doesn't wipe out. He instead redeems! He sends Jesus to pay the debt for our sin and to reveal the coming of the kingdom. We are invited into the very newness of God. There is a new world a-coming and we are part of it. That is the promise for all eternity. That is the definition of eternity. God is making all things new.

Those are some of the promises in Revelation. There are more and we will look at them as we read on. This book of Revelation is God's promise, God's hope, for you.

QUESTIONS

1. How do you see the book of Revelation? What words would you use to describe your impressions of it?
2. Have you ever heard of Revelation being a book of promise?
3. Given the promises that we've listed, which seem the most powerful to you? Why?
4. What might it mean for you to say that we will be before the throne of God?
5. How does being God's people shape our lives?
6. What questions do you have about the book of Revelation?

Section 2

The Risen Jesus

LET'S MOVE INTO SOME of the specific passages of Revelation, and let's begin our work where John (the author) begins—namely, the opening chapter. The first chapter of Revelation is dominated by a vision of the risen Jesus. It is a rich, provocative, and, yes, confusing picture of the Lord. We are shown the glorified and living One, the reigning Lord of heaven and earth. Yet there are details here that are hard to grasp. This is an image we have to explore.

Just a quick point as we begin, please note how John begins the book of Revelation. He points to Jesus. The very first line in the book is, "The revelation of Jesus Christ." Most of our modern Bibles put a title on this last book of the Bible. Our modern Bibles call this book "The Revelation to John." That title is a later addition. John's first words focus squarely on Jesus. To further reinforce his point, in chapter 1 John includes a detailed, rich description of Jesus in all his resurrected glory. John is very clear, this book is about Jesus Christ. We need to hear that in our modern day. We have a tendency in our modern day to reduce Revelation to some sort of futuristic road map to the end of history. We read the book to discover what will happen between now and the time of Jesus' return. But that isn't John's focus. John clearly says this is a revelation of Jesus Christ. We do well to let John guide us as we read what He has to say.

So, let's begin with John's image of Jesus in chapter 1. Here is what John writes:

> Then I turned to see whose voice it was that spoke to me, and on turning I saw seven golden lampstands, and in the midst of the lampstands I saw one like the Son of Man, clothed with a long robe and with a golden sash across his chest. His head and his hair were white as white wool, white as snow; his eyes were like a flame of fire, his feet were like burnished bronze, refined as in a furnace, and his voice was like the sound of many waters. In his right hand he held seven stars, and from his mouth came a sharp, two-edged sword, and his face was like the sun shining with full force.
>
> When I saw him, I fell at his feet as though dead. But he placed his right hand on me, saying, "Do not be afraid; I am the first and the last, and the living one. I was dead, and see, I am alive forever and ever; and I have the keys of Death and of Hades." (1:12–18)

John begins by writing that he heard a voice addressing him, so he turns to the voice and finds himself face-to-face with Jesus. John writes that Jesus is standing in the midst of seven golden lampstands. What are the lampstands? They are a symbol for the seven congregations that Revelation is addressed to. How do we know that? John tells us; in v. 20 of this first chapter, John writes that the seven lampstands are the seven churches. By the way, that is an incredibly important point. Where is Jesus? In the midst of his churches. Jesus will never forsake his people. When Christians gather together, it is always in the presence of the risen Lord. That was true for the congregations addressed in Revelation; that is true for us today.

John then goes on in v. 13 to begin describing Jesus. It is rich, highly symbolic language, drawn from the Old Testament. Let's look at the images:

- Jesus is "one like a son of man"—this image is drawn from Dan 7:13. The book of Daniel looked for a heaven-sent deliverer, called the son of man, to save God's people. John says this Old Testament promise is fulfilled in Jesus.

The Risen Jesus

- He is "clothed with a long robe and with a golden sash around his chest." This is clothing of high social stature and might. Perhaps John is echoing the priestly garments of Exod 28:4 and Jesus is proclaimed as the great high priest, the ultimate mediator between God and humanity.

- "The hairs of his head were white, like white wool, like snow." This is also taken from Dan 7 (v. 9). In Daniel God is described as the Ancient of Days; Daniel writes that the clothing of the Ancient of Days was as "white as snow" and "the hair of his head was like pure wool." John is drawing on this imagery; when John writes that Jesus' hair is white like snow, he is telling us that Jesus is to be identified with the Ancient of Days or, in other words, God! This Jesus is of the very nature of the Almighty!

- "His eyes were like a flame of fire, his feet were like burnished bronze, refined in a furnace, and his voice was like the roar of many waters." John now draws from Dan 10:5–6 to continue his picture of Jesus. Let your imaginations play with these images. Jesus has eyes like flames of fire, full of life with a burning, penetrating gaze. His feet were like burnished, or perhaps shining, bronze, indicating power and majesty. Jesus' voice was like the sound of many waters; imagine a voice as rich as the roar of rapids or a raging ocean. John is stretching our imaginations to give us a sense of Jesus' glory.

- "From his mouth came a sharp two-edged sword." In Isa 49:2 the sword represents the word of God. John is telling us it is from the lips of Jesus that we most clearly hear the word of God. In fact we can go even further and say that this Jesus is the Word of God!

- "His face was like the sun shining in full strength." Again an echo of Dan 10:6, Jesus as the risen Lord is described as glowing in the wonder and majesty of who his is.

What we have in these lines are images of the power and glory of the Savior. This is the Son of God Himself! We do well to simply let our minds soar in the wonder of the Lord.

Notice please the language that John is using. It is language of "like" and "as." John has a challenge. How does he describe Jesus in his full glory? The challenge is, there isn't adequate human language to do so. So John uses language of symbolism and imagination. John is an artist who uses words to paint pictures, pictures that gives us a feel for the glory and wonder of Jesus. We can take this language apart and analyze it, as we have just done, and that is appropriate. But we also need to step back to visualize and sense what John is sharing. John wants us to encounter and experience the greatest truth of life—that Jesus is the glorified, risen Lord![1]

Let me note another point that is important for us to understand. Notice how John uses symbols. He uses symbols to speak of and point to deeper realities. We ought not to take the symbols literally, but rather ask what John is saying by using the symbols. For example, when John says that Jesus has white hair, John isn't saying that Jesus is prematurely gray.[2] Rather he is saying that Jesus is the Ancient of Days—namely, He is to be identified with God Himself. Or when John says that Jesus has a sword in his mouth, don't think of a literal dagger between Jesus' teeth. The symbol, rather, helps us understand that Jesus is the one who most truly speaks the word of God.

When we deal with symbols in Revelation, we need to ask what the symbols mean. Don't take the symbols literally, rather, ask what they say. This is rather easy to see here in chapter 1, but we need to remember this later in the book when we get to language of things like Armageddon and the one thousand-year reign. Those too are symbols, and we need to read them as such. The question in reading Revelation is, What are the symbols saying?

One more important point, don't think that because John uses symbols, he isn't writing the truth. Quite the contrary, John uses symbols and images to proclaim the deepest truths of life, truths that often exceed what we can say in non-symbolic language. For example, when John's symbols proclaim that Jesus is of God, and

---

1. I deal with this material in a similar manner in my book *Come, Lord Jesus*, 19–21.

2. Metzger, *Breaking the Code*, 27.

that Jesus speaks the word of God, those points are deeply, deeply true. John uses symbols to proclaim and help us see the truth of what God is about.

John concludes his picture of Jesus by writing that he falls "at his [Jesus'] feet as though dead." I have to think that is an appropriate response to seeing the Savior in his full glory! I'm sure John was terrified, overwhelmed. But Jesus lovingly reaches out to John, touches him, and says, "Don't be afraid." Isn't that marvelous? This glorified One, this Lord of the cosmos, is also the one who reaches out to us, touches us, comforts us. He is the one who loves us through all of life! Jesus tells John (and us!) that Jesus is the living one; He died but has risen and lives forever. Jesus is saying that we can trust Him totally, for nothing, not even death, can stop his love for us. Jesus then adds He has the keys of death and Hades. When we face the death of loved ones, when we face our own deaths, Jesus is the one who will set us free—again, a beautiful, powerful image of truth and life.

John begins Revelation with this powerful picture of Jesus. It is John's way of telling us that this book is about Jesus. It is John's way of telling us that we need to know Jesus! We read Revelation to see and encounter the living Lord, the Lord who reaches out to you and me!

QUESTIONS

1. Did you realize that Revelation is first and foremost a book about Jesus? Too often we try to reduce Revelation to being a road map to the future, and we ignore the real focus of the book. How might realizing this book is about Jesus influence how you read the book?

2. John wants us to know that Jesus is in the midst of his churches. Where would you say that Jesus is? Have you experienced Jesus in the midst of the church?

3. Why do you think that John uses all this symbolic language?

4. What might it be like to see Jesus in his full glory?

5. John wants us to see more of who Jesus is. What questions do you have about Jesus?
6. Of all the images shared here about Jesus, which one seems to you the most helpful?

Section 3

The Congregation in Ephesus
A Less Than Loving Faith

HAVE YOU EVER BEEN in a congregation where the people don't like each other? You walk in for a worship service on a Sunday morning and you very quickly get the sense that something isn't right? There is tension, an uncomfortable atmosphere. You can feel it, sense it; people are just uneasy with each other. You don't know what the issue is, but you know that these people don't get along.

Unfortunately there are too many congregations in our modern day that are like that. The book of Revelation is addressed to a congregation that was like that two thousand years ago. One of the congregations to which Revelation was originally addressed was a congregation in the city of Ephesus. John writes about and to this congregation in 2:1–7. This congregation fits the above description all too well.

For some background, Ephesus was the largest city in ancient Asia Minor; it was a busy seaport with a population of around a quarter of a million people. There was a large and elaborate temple in Ephesus dedicated to the worship of the pagan goddess Artemis, who was claimed by Ephesus as their special deity. There had been a Christian congregation in Ephesus for probably fifty years by the time John wrote Revelation. We know that Paul had spent three years in Ephesus, working with Christians.

Engaging Revelation

At the beginning of chapter 2, John has a message for this congregation in Ephesus.[1] By way of background, in chapters 2 and 3 of Revelation, John has messages for seven specific congregations in what is now Asia Minor or Turkey. He addresses each of the seven congregations individually and begins with the congregation in Ephesus. Here is what John writes:

> These are the words of him who holds the seven stars in his right hand, who walks among the seven golden lampstands:
>
> I know your works, your toil and your patient endurance. I know that you cannot tolerate evildoers; you have tested those who claim to be apostles but are not, and have found them to be false. I also know that you are enduring patiently and bearing up for the sake of my name, and that you have not grown weary. But I have this against you, that you have abandoned the love you had at first. Remember then from what you have fallen; repent, and do the works you did at first. If not, I will come to you and remove your lampstand from its place, unless you repent. Yet this is to your credit: you hate the works of the Nicolaitans, which I also hate. Let anyone who has an ear listen to what the Spirit is saying to the churches. To everyone who conquers, I will give permission to eat from the tree of life that is in the paradise of God. (2:1–7)

Please note how John has words of both commendation and correction for this congregation. He begins with commendation. The congregation has been faithful in the midst of doctrinal disputes. There have been false teachers in Ephesus and the congregation has been presented with false doctrine. They have wrestled over this. The congregation has held to correct teachings. They have worked at it, they have struggled; it hasn't been easy. Nonetheless, even with the temptations of false teachings, they have remained true. John commends them for that.

---

1. I should comment on how I understand the authorship of Revelation. I will usually refer to John as the author; at other times I'll refer to Jesus as the author. Both are correct. It was John who actually wrote the words of the book. John is also clear, this is Jesus' message, given to John by Jesus to be shared with the seven congregations. The message of Revelation is finally Jesus' message.

The Congregation in Ephesus

John goes further. He commends the congregation for their patient endurance, bearing up for Jesus' name's sake and not growing weary in all that they have faced. I can't imagine it was easy to be a small Christian community in the midst of a pagan and hostile culture. Quite the contrary, I suspect following Jesus meant struggle and toil and opposition. These Christians have fought those battles and remained faithful. There is much to admire in this congregation.

But their faithfulness has come at a cost. They have "abandoned the love [they] had at first" (2:4). In the midst of the struggles and challenges, they have turned cold. Their care for each other has waned. It seems that their obedience to true teaching has come at the price of love for one another.

John is clear, this is unacceptable. Christians are to adhere to true doctrine, of course. They also need to love each other. These aren't either/or categories. The Lord to whom they are faithful also directs them to love for one another. Both faithful teaching and love of neighbor are essential to the life of faith, and the Christians in Ephesus are directed to reclaim the love they have left behind.

At this point the book of Revelation has something powerful to say to our modern day. Both faithfulness to correct teachings and love of neighbor must be lifted up in the church. One cannot be restricted for the other.

I fear we live in a day when too many congregations and denominations and Christians have followed the path of Ephesus. Like Ephesus we do struggle with false teachings in our day. The church of every age has had to deal with that; in actuality I fear that our modern day deals with more than its share of falsehoods and distortions. Moreover, faithfulness takes a lot of work as we live in this increasingly non-Christian and hostile culture of ours. But that can never be an excuse for failing to love others. Too often in our day Christians engage in struggles to be doctrinally correct, and in the process we become rigid, hard, and unwilling or unable to care about people. We lose sight of loving one another; we grow defensive, harsh. Church members get mad at each other, congregations grow cold, denominations treat each other in disparaging ways. Like Ephesus doctrinal truth and correctness come at the price of love.

In Revelation John reminds us that love is always essential. Of course we have to continually work to be faithful and true in our teachings. We also are a people of love and grace. We follow the God of love, and the church is defined by the Lord who loved even his enemies. This Lord is clear, we are to "love one another as he has loved us" (John 15:12). This love of Christ needs to overflow always and especially in the church. In fact, particularly when we disagree with other Christians, we need to look at them anew with the eyes of compassion as given us by Jesus.

There is no substitute for love. As a people loved by Christ, we are to love others. That love is always to be shared in the Christian community. The church by its very nature must be a place of compassion, forgiveness, mercy, generosity. As John reminds us, to do anything less is to sacrifice our identity as Christ's people.

Revelation was written nearly two thousand years ago and was originally addressed to congregations half a world away from us. Yet the message of Revelation is so vital for our modern day. That is the wonder of God's word, it continually and always speaks to people of each new generation. May we follow that word in love for our neighbors!

We are called to both faithful teaching and to love of one another. These can never be either/or categories. Both are essential as we follow the Lord of truth and love.

QUESTIONS

1. Have you ever been in a congregation like the one in Ephesus, one that feels cold and divided? What was that like? Was the congregation able to address that?
2. What does love in a congregation look like, feel like?
3. Do you see the church as struggling with false teachings in our day?
4. Do we live in a hostile culture?

5. What might we do to make our congregations more loving?
6. What would Jesus commend in your congregation? What would Jesus correct?

Section 4

The Congregation in Pergamum
Called to Be Distinctively Different

IN THIS SECTION I want to look at the message to the congregation in Pergamum. Before doing so, let me share a bit of background information on chapters 2 and 3 in Revelation.

Chapters 2 and 3 contain what we usually call the messages to the seven congregations; we've looked already at the message to the congregation in Ephesus. The book of Revelation (or maybe better, the letter that we call Revelation) is specifically addressed to seven first-century congregations in what is now modern-day Turkey. In chapters 2 and 3 there are specific messages to each congregation.

Every time I read these messages, I'm struck by three things: First, by how well John knows these congregations. I suspect he had a pastoral relationship with these congregations. He knows them well, strengthens and weaknesses. Second, I am struck by how appropriate and important these ancient messages still are to modern-day congregations. These seven ancient congregations share in issues that continue in congregations of our day, and we need to hear these messages. Third, I am struck by how foundational chapters 2 and 3 are for the rest of the book. The issues that John raises in chapters 2 and 3 will be addressed throughout the remainder of the book of Revelation.

The Congregation in Pergamum

That is just a bit of background; with that let's move on to the message to the congregation in Pergamum. The message to Pergamum is found in 2:12–17. Here is what John writes:

> These are the words of him who has the sharp two-edged sword:
>
> I know where you are living, where Satan's throne is. Yet you are holding fast to my name, and you did not deny your faith in me even in the days of Antipas my witness, my faithful one, who was killed among you, where Satan lives. But I have a few things against you: you have some there who hold to the teaching of Balaam, who taught Balak to put a stumbling block before the people of Israel, so that they would eat food sacrificed to idols and practice fornication. So you also have some who hold to the teaching of the Nicolaitans. Repent then. If not, I will come to you soon and make war against them with the sword of my mouth. Let anyone who has an ear listen to what the Spirit is saying to the churches. To everyone who conquers I will give some of the hidden manna, and I will give a white stone, and on the white stone is written a new name that no one knows except the one who receives it.

John again begins with words of commendation. The Christians in Pergamum have held fast to the faith even in a hostile and unaccepting city. In fact one of the members, a man named Antipas, has been killed for the faith. The Christians have been faithful even in the midst of opposition, and they are commended for that.

But there is a problem. Jesus has "a few things against them" (2:14). The congregation has members who are saying that it is permissible for Christians to "eat food sacrificed to idols and practice fornication" (2:14). That sounds a bit strange to our modern ears. Let's see what the issues are.

The first is eating food that has been sacrificed to idols. That suggests all sorts of strange images to our minds, particularly of pagan worship. The reality was a bit more complicated. In the ancient world, the temples of various deities served as slaughterhouses. Cattle and livestock were brought to the temples; the animals would be slaughtered there and part of the meat would be offered in honor of the god or goddess. The rest of the meat was sold for public consumption. Because part of the meat had been given in offering, all the meat was considered sanctified. Much if not all of the meat available in a city would come through this process; it would have been quite difficult to find meat that hadn't been offered to an idol. If you wanted meat, you probably would get it from a temple. To complicate things further, civic groups like trade guilds or civic organizations would certainly get their meat through the local temples.[1] The question became, could Christians eat meat that had been obtained through this process?

John, in this message to Pergamum, lists his opponents as those "who hold to the teaching of the Nicolaitans." It is a good assumption that the Nicolaitans were teaching something to the effect of—go ahead and eat the meat. The Nicolaitans could argue, don't worry about where the meat comes from. Even if it came from a temple, you know that idols have no real existence. Just eat whatever is served and don't worry about it. The Nicolaitans could argue that Christians need to be involved in civic meals and affairs; how else could Christians make connections for evangelism? In fact the Nicolaitans could even appeal to the apostle Paul who at least gives some leeway for eating meat offered to idols in 1 Cor 8.

The second item that John lists is fornication. That could mean sexual encounters outside of marriage. But more likely it refers to worshiping other gods. In the Old Testament worshiping other gods is often referred to as fornication or sexual immorality.[2] It most likely means the same here. The issue is actually an issue of worshiping the Roman emperor.

In the Roman Empire of the time, and particularly in the eastern parts of the empire, which included Pergamum, there was a growing practice of deifying the emperor. The emperor would be referred to as "lord and god," temples were erected to the emperor, and coins would proclaim the emperor as a deity. Citizens were

---

1. Koester, *Revelation and the End*, 58–61.
2. Koester, *Revelation and the End*, 62.

expected to offer incense at the emperor's temple and say something like "Caesar is Lord."

Now what is interesting about this is that many of the Romans, and some of the Roman emperors, didn't take this at all seriously. The practice of emperor deification originated, not with the Roman emperors, but in cities and among local leaders in the eastern part of the Roman Empire. It originated among people who hoped to win the emperor's favor, which certainly held political and monetary advantages. We know that some Roman emperors did encourage the practice, but others thought it rather frivolous. Many Romans didn't see anything serious about the practice. Most of the Romans were polytheists, so adding another god didn't matter.[3] To go even further, saying "Caesar is Lord" was often seen as more of a pledge of allegiance to the empire than a religious statement. To not say that "Caesar is Lord" would raise questions of your loyalty to the state.

What were the Christians to do? Again we suspect that the Nicolaitans argued something to the effect of "just get along." Offer the emperor a pinch of incense, say what you need to. The Nicolaitans could argue, it is no big deal. We know that the emperor is only a man, just do what you need to do to function in the culture of Pergamum.

In both of these cases, the Nicolaitans were arguing for what we call assimilation. The idea is that Christians should get along with the culture in which they live. Christians are to be good citizens of the state, participating in the culture and doing all that the culture requires. Christianity was in effect merged with cultural beliefs and practices.

In Revelation John says no. John draws a line and says that Christians cannot and must not compromise on matters of faith. For John it is clear, if meat has been offered to an idol, Christians are to avoid it. In addition, no one is to be addressed as Lord except for Jesus Christ. For John the issue is clear, Christians do not compromise on how they live and express their faith.

3. Koester, *Revelation*, 365–66.

For John following Jesus meant living a life that was distinctively different from the ways of the world. Christians were not to compromise on that. Christians were to bear witness to Jesus by their words and their actions, and compromising with a pagan culture was not acceptable.

As we jump the years from Revelation to our modern day, this issue of assimilation is still with us. In fact it is at least as challenging a question for us as it was for the early Christians in Pergamum. Where can we as Christians live with the values of our culture, and where do we need to oppose cultural values for the sake of our faith?

I believe this is becoming more and more of a pointed question for American Christians. A generation ago we assumed that America was a Christian culture. (I don't know if that assumption was ever totally accurate, but we assumed it was.) Now we live in a time when the values of our culture frequently head in one direction and Jesus directs us in another. We as American Christians need to make decisions like the Christians in ancient Pergamum. Where can we affirm and live with the values of our culture, and where do we oppose them?

Let me share a few examples where I see our culture opposing the values of faith:

- We live in a culture of sexualization. Sex sells in our day; it is prominent in everything from pornography to advertising. Hard-core pornography is rampant; even closer to home we watch movies and even television commercials that are much more graphic than is necessary or acceptable. I can see a lot of lingerie, body parts, and intimate encounters just watching a movie on TV. I'm sure it's not what the good Lord intended for our sexuality.

- We live in a culture of materialism, where wealth is central and buying and possessing is key. We value money! Jesus points us in a different direction and tells us we can't serve God and wealth.

The Congregation in Pergamum

- We live in a pluralistic culture that says that all ways and thoughts are equally valid. The culture says there is no one, eternal truth; all approaches are valid. In fact we define what is true for ourselves. Jesus points us in a different way and says He alone is the way, the truth, and the life.
- We live in a polarized culture where we disdain and even attack those who differ from us. Jesus again points us in a different way and calls us to be agents of reconciliation and community.

This list can go on and on: how we value human life, how we understand marriage, how we order our priorities, how we care for God's creation; our Christians values more and more put us at odds with our culture.

We find ourselves in the position of the early Christians in Pergamum. We wrestle with the question: What does faithfulness to Jesus require of us? There are those who still teach in line with the Nicolaitans, arguing that we should just get along, perhaps even water down the faith a bit. I believe that the Church needs to listen to the teaching of John. We need to be clear on what our faith calls us to do and dare to live distinctively for Jesus. That is part of the witness that Revelation and the entire New Testament call us to share.

Please note, this is not going to be easy. I fear it will be dangerous, as it was for the Christians in Pergamum. We as Christians will be out of step with what is accepted and popular. We will be open for ridicule and even persecution. But it is the only way we can be faithful to the Lord who has overcome this world.

John directs all who follow Jesus Christ to dare to live for Jesus in an unfaithful world. Let me also note, doing this is part of our witness as Christians. Our differences with the world call attention to the God who leads in a different way of life. One of my friends likes to say, we live in a day when lots of folks don't have God on their radar screen. Too many people in our day aren't aware of God and don't think in terms of God. As we as Christians live lives that are distinctively different, we bear witness to the God who leads in a richer way of life. Perhaps our "differentness" can help people to see beyond the ways of this world to a deeper reality, that of the Lord who is making all things new.

I mentioned at the beginning of this section how the issues raised in Revelation continue to be issues that our modern day and modern church struggle with. That is certainly true with the question of assimilation. There are plenty of voices in our day that sound like the ancient Nicolaitans, calling for Christians to merge into and get along with the ways of the world. May we have the courage and faith to dare to live for Jesus!

QUESTIONS

1. Do you see American culture and the Christian faith going in different directions? What are some examples that you see?
2. How do we deal with American culture and Christianity going in different directions? How do we be sure we are being faithful to Jesus?
3. Do you sense more opposition to Christianity in our day?
4. Are there those in the modern church who teach the way of the Nicolaitans—namely, just get along with the culture?
5. How might we respond to those who disagree and differ from us?
6. How might we be "distinctively different" from our culture?

Section 5

The Congregation in Laodicea
A Lukewarm Faith

I HAVE TO CONFESS that the message to Laodicea is my favorite of the messages in chapters 2 and 3. It is pointed and direct; John doesn't pull any punches. It is colorful and challenges a congregation that doesn't want to be challenged. I believe it is the message I most need to hear!

The message to Laodicea is the last of the seven messages, found in 3:14-22. Here is what John writes:

> The words of the Amen, the faithful and true witness, the origin of God's creation:
>
> I know your works; you are neither cold nor hot. I wish that you were either cold or hot. So, because you are lukewarm, and neither cold nor hot, I am about to spit you out of my mouth. For you say, "I am rich, I have prospered, and I need nothing." You do not realize that you are wretched, pitiable, poor, blind, and naked. Therefore I counsel you to buy from me gold refined by fire so that you may be rich; and white robes to clothe you and to keep the shame of your nakedness from being seen; and salve to anoint your eyes so that you may see. I reprove and discipline those whom I love. Be earnest, therefore, and repent. Listen! I am standing at the door, knocking; if you hear my voice and open the door, I will

come in to you and eat with you, and you with me. To the one who conquers I will give a place with me on my throne, just as I myself conquered and sat down with my Father on his throne. Let anyone who has an ear listen to what the Spirit is saying to the churches.

Laodicea was a wealthy city. It was renowned as a financial center; it had a medical school with a famous eye salve and a textile industry that included a valuable black wool. Laodicea was so wealthy that when it was damaged by an earthquake in AD 60, it declined to accept Roman aid to rebuild. (When was the last time you heard of a municipality that declined government assistance?) We assume the Christian congregation in Laodicea fit in with the rest of the community. As we listen to John's description of the congregation, it seems that they too were wealthy and content.

John accuses the congregation of being lukewarm in their faith. We suspect that their wealth led them to believe they were self-sufficient. They were affluent, successful, benefiting from the commerce that the Roman Empire supported, probably enjoying the protection and ways of Rome. Given all that, they did not see themselves as in great need of God. Most likely they had a place for God in their lives, but it was not central. Wealth can be a dangerous detriment to faith.

John writes that in their pride the congregation sees themselves as a model for faith; they can't see the trouble they are in. John critiques them in scathing terms, drawing from the local circumstances of Laodicea to make his point. The congregation says they are rich, probably thinking both materially and spiritually. John tells them they are "wretched, pitiable, poor," needing to buy the true riches that only Jesus can provide (3:17–18). John goes on and writes, you have a rich textile industry, but before God you stand naked (3:18). This community has a medical school and eye salve, but spiritually it is blind and doesn't even know it (3:18). Jesus goes so far as to threaten, in light of Laodicea's lukewarmness in faith, to spit them out of his mouth (3:16). (Let the harshness and impact of that imagery sink in for a moment!) It is a devastating critique of a congregation that holds itself in high regard.

The Congregation in Laodicea

I mentioned earlier that I'm fascinated with this message to Laodicea, and the reason for this is that, in many ways, I think I live in Laodicea. Oh, not literally, of course. But the circumstances that John describes are so accurate for congregations I've been part of. If I'm honest, these critiques are accurate critiques of my own life of faith. I'm not rich by American standards, but I'm very comfortable. I'm well-clothed and fed, I have 401ks and insurance policies and a nice home and retirement plan. I too often live with the illusion that I'm self-sufficient and self-established. I take credit for my own life and I lose my sense that in reality I am totally dependent on God, and all that I have is a gift from Him. In my supposed self-sufficiency I get complacent and lose sight of my need for a Savior. I think I'd fit in well at Laodicea, and I fear there is a lot of that going around in American Christianity.

The congregation at Laodicea needs a wake-up call and John provides that. He points out that they aren't nearly as secure and self-sufficient as they like to believe. In fact there are gaping holes in their life. John challenges the Christians and tells them to get beyond themselves and look again to the Savior. I wonder sometimes how the congregation at Laodicea reacted when this letter of Revelation was first read to them! I suspect they were horrified, angry, and offended. I've often wondered if John's words sunk in.

Then, toward the end of this message, comes a piece of good news. Jesus in beautiful imagery says that He stands at the door knocking (3:20). He is asking that the people of Laodicea invite Him in and share again in his fellowship. Jesus hasn't given up on this congregation. In spite of their pride, supposed self-sufficiency, and lukewarm faith, Jesus hasn't given up. Instead He knocks, inviting them to renewal and true life.

That is good news for us also. For those of us who suspect that we live in Laodicea-like circumstances, John provides this wakeup call for us. He challenges us to be honest about who we are and about our need for God. He challenges us to be honest about our lives, including our shortsightedness, self focus, and lack of faith. And then he reminds us of the Savior who knocks for us also. Jesus, in a grace beyond our understanding, still calls for us. Incredible news, lifegiving news! Jesus hasn't given up. Will we hear his call?

QUESTIONS

1. Given what Revelation says, what do you think life was like in ancient Laodicea? What do you think the congregation in Laodicea was like?
2. Do you know of any modern congregations that sound like this congregation in Laodicea?
3. What might it mean when Jesus says He "is about to spit the congregation out of his mouth"?
4. Is our culture spiritually blind? Do wealth and affluence blind us to God?
5. Are there times when you overlook or ignore your dependency on God?
6. Has anyone challenged you or provided a wake-up call for you in the faith? How did you respond?
7. Jesus knocks at the door for us also. How might we open the door to Him?

Section 6

There Is a Throne

WE LIVE IN A strange age. Perhaps every age can say that, but ours seems particularly weird and empty. People have come to think that there isn't any real or lasting purpose to life. We are "postmoderns," as we call ourselves, and that means no absolutes. No lasting values, no hope in anything beyond ourselves, no faith in ultimate promises. The idea of a God just doesn't seem relevant, possible, or worthwhile. Too often people can't even be bothered with the question of whether or not there is an Almighty One. Life is just what we create it to be.

Revelation explodes upon us with a whole different view. In proclamations and images that stagger our minds, Revelation announces there is purpose and direction and meaning. There is hope. Why? Because at the center of the universe is God.

Revelation makes this radical announcement in chapter 4. With John we are ushered into the throne room of God and given a sense of the creator. John creates a picture that blasts away at our modern, limited views, and opens us to the wonder and power of God.

Here is what John writes:

> At once I was in the spirit, and there in heaven stood a throne, with one seated on the throne! And the one

seated there looks like jasper and cornelian, and around the throne is a rainbow that looks like an emerald. Around the throne are twenty-four thrones, and seated on the thrones are twenty-four elders, dressed in white robes, with golden crowns on their heads. Coming from the throne are flashes of lightning, and rumblings and peals of thunder, and in front of the throne burn seven flaming torches, which are the seven spirits of God; and in front of the throne there is something like a sea of glass, like crystal.

Around the throne, and on each side of the throne, are four living creatures, full of eyes in front and behind: the first living creature like a lion, the second living creature like an ox, the third living creature with a face like a human face, and the fourth living creature like a flying eagle. And the four living creatures, each of them with six wings, are full of eyes all around and inside. Day and night without ceasing they sing,

"Holy, holy, holy,
the Lord God the Almighty,
   who was and is and is to come."

And whenever the living creatures give glory and honor and thanks to the one who is seated on the throne, who lives forever and ever, the twenty-four elders fall before the one who is seated on the throne and worship the one who lives forever and ever; they cast their crowns before the throne, singing,

"You are worthy, our Lord and God,
   to receive glory and honor and power,
for you created all things,
   and by your will they existed and were created." (4:2–11)

In chapters 2 and 3 of Revelation John has been addressing seven congregations here on earth. Now in chapter 4 he is caught up into heaven. He finds himself in the throne room of God. John begins simply enough: "There in heaven stood a throne, with one seated on the throne." Those simple words convey the deepest, most transformative message for life. The world is given in God! At the center of the universe, at the center of reality, is God. Life is not some hopeless mishmash of random beings trying to get by. It is rooted in, given by, and directed to God. All of a sudden there is the possibility of direction, meaning, purpose, value, hope! There is an ultimate one, and He is guiding this planet!

John is clear. At the center of the universe there is a throne. For his ancient contemporaries, John is also clear, this throne is not occupied by the Roman emperor. We might add in our modern-day, it is not surrounded by American flags. The throne belongs to God. The clear implications of this is that life is rooted in and directed to this Lord.

John makes this powerful assertion, then he goes on to tell us some things about God. John begins by saying that God has the appearance of jasper and carnelian. (Just a note, much of John's imagery here comes from Ezek 1.) Jasper and carnelian are shining, precious gems. John is suggesting that there is a glow that emanates from the throne, a sign of power and wonder. Moreover, around the throne there is "a rainbow that had the appearance of an emerald." At this point we have to stop and let our imaginations go to work. A rainbow glowing like an emerald? Try to picture that. I can't get my mind around that, and that is John's point. He is stretching our imaginations to proclaim the sheer majesty of God.

John then goes on and notes that around the throne are twenty-four thrones, on which were seated twenty-four elders. Just a note on John's writing here, he is developing a picture of God as the center of reality, and everything that exists emanates from God. Elders, angels, living creatures, human beings, all of creation is centered in God! With the twenty-four elders John is developing the idea of a heavenly court. Why twenty-four elders? We aren't sure. Perhaps they represent an Old Testament council of angels, perhaps twenty-four comes from adding the twelve sons of Jacob with the twelve apostles. The point is that creation is centered in the Almighty who is seated on the throne.

Please note, we may have a bit of political satire here. We think in our modern day that religion and politics must always be separated. John knows of no such boundaries. All of life, including politics and government, is subject to God and so John takes a poke at Roman propaganda here. The Romans proclaimed that the center of the world is the throne of Caesar in Rome. Caesar's throne was surrounded by elders or authorities or subject kings. John is not so subtly letting his readers know that anything that Caesar has can't hold a candle to what God is about. The Roman throne is just a pale imitation of the real power that is in heaven.

John goes on—lightning and thunder come from the throne. They remind us of the power, and yes the danger, of God. Seven spirits of God (perhaps seven, being a number of completion, is to remind us of the one, full, Holy Spirit of God!) surround the throne. Before the throne is a sea of glass, like crystal. In the Old Testament the sea is often a symbol of chaos and threat. But here in God's presence it is calm as glass.

This is a picture of glory! As we look at all these images, we need to explain and analyze them. But more importantly, we need to step back and simply sense the wonder and glory of all this. John is using evocative and picturesque language to give us a sense of the power and majesty of God. There is a God and He is majestic above anything we can fathom or understand. We need to let our imaginations run with all of this and simply be swept up in the glory of God.

John is giving us an alternative to the poverty of our modern worldview. We too often think we live in a world that is empty of God. It is a world that is ultimately meaningless and hopeless. John gives us a different picture. John announces a world given in God, a world created by the hand of One far greater than we can ever imagine. It is a world endowed with dignity and depth beyond our human view. Yes, John is well aware that this world has been marred by sin. He knows full well the damage that we have done to God's creation and to ourselves. But John knows the victory of Jesus Christ that reclaims this planet and thereby affirms and celebrates the dignity and glory that God bestows. This is a picture that our modern world is literally dying to hear!

John goes on. On each side of the throne are living creatures, described as a lion, an ox, a human, and an eagle. All of creation is centered in and comes from God. These living creatures are full of eyes, indicating that God knows what is going on in his creation. The living creatures are described as having six wings, an Old Testament reference from Isa 6:2 of heavenly creatures surrounding the throne of God. Day and night they worship God, a reminder that all of creation is involved in the praise of its creator! When the living creatures worship, the twenty-four elders fall down and worship also, casting their crowns before the Almighty. This image has been captured in hymns as ancient as "Crown Him with Many Crowns" and as modern as Chris Tomlin's "Casting Crowns." The proclamation is of all creation erupting in worship of God. In fact, woven into these images is the invitation for us to come and join in. Perhaps the best response to seeing all of this is to join in the chorus of praise!

Let's return to where we started—"There in heaven stood a throne, with one seated on the throne." That announcement is so simple, so basic, yet so essential for our modern day. There is a God, a Lord of this universe. Incredibly, He is a God of grace and love for all that He has made, and that includes you! We are invited into his newness and hope. We are invited to the very throne of God. How foolish, how shortsighted we are if we miss this opportunity.

QUESTIONS

1. Do you see God as the center of reality? What does that mean for your life?

2. There is a tendency in our day to call ourselves "post-moderns" who believe in nothing absolute and who recognize no permanent values. Do you have things that you believe to be absolute and permanent? What are they?

3. John uses images of gems and a heavenly court and thunder and lightning to describe the glory of God. Are those images helpful for you? How would you describe the glory of God?

4. As you try to visualize God's throne room in your imagination, what do you see?

5. John is most likely writing some political satire about the Roman rule. Is it appropriate for faith to critique the government?

6. Again, John's point is that the world and life are given in God. How can that shape and deepen our lives? How do we share that with our modern day?

Section 7

The Lion and the Lamb
Or Better—The Lion Is the Lamb!

JOHN HAS A REMARKABLE ability to surprise us. As we read his work, he keeps heading off in directions we don't expect. We think he is going to zig; instead he zags. Revelation has a knack for keeping us wondering.

One of the places where this is the most obvious is in chapter 5. John is promised a messiah who is a lion. He is promised "the Lion of the tribe of Judah, the Root of David" (v. 5)! And then John sees—a lamb. A lamb! He is looking for a lion, he sees a lamb. We have to first sense the shock of this, and then ask what in the world all this means.

Let's do some digging. Here is the actual passage:

> Then I saw in the right hand of the one seated on the throne a scroll written on the inside and on the back, sealed with seven seals; and I saw a mighty angel proclaiming with a loud voice, "Who is worthy to open the scroll and break its seals?" And no one in heaven or on earth or under the earth was able to open the scroll or to look into it. And I began to weep bitterly because no one was found worthy to open the scroll or to look into it. Then one of the elders said to me, "Do not weep. See, the Lion of the tribe of Judah, the Root of David, has conquered, so that he can open the scroll and its seven seals."

Then I saw between the throne and the four living creatures and among the elders a Lamb standing as if it had been slaughtered, having seven horns and seven eyes, which are the seven spirits of God sent out into all the earth. He went and took the scroll from the right hand of the one who was seated on the throne. When he had taken the scroll, the four living creatures and the twenty-four elders fell before the Lamb, each holding a harp and golden bowls full of incense, which are the prayers of the saints. They sing a new song:

"You are worthy to take the scroll
    and to open its seals,
for you were slaughtered and by your blood you ransomed for God
    saints from every tribe and language and people and nation;
you have made them to be a kingdom and priests serving our God,
    and they will reign on earth." (5:1–10)

In chapter 4 John has introduced his vision of the heavenly throne room. Now in chapter 5 John continues with this vision. John sees God on the throne; then he sees in the hand of God a sealed scroll. This scroll seems to contain God's plan for the world; in fact as we will see, as the seals are opened, the plan is enacted. But an angel asks, "Who is worthy to open the scroll?" It's a fair question. Who is worthy to bring about God's plan for the world? I'm certainly not. I suspect you aren't either. John quickly realizes that no one on heaven or earth is able to fulfill God's plan of redemption.

John begins to weep because the scroll won't be opened. Then one of the elders says, "Do not weep. See, the Lion of the tribe of Judah, the Root of David, has conquered, so that he can open the scroll and its seven seals." Note carefully what is being said here. The elder is saying that God's own messiah will open the scroll and redeem the world. The language is right out of the Old Testament and right out of Jewish expectations for the messiah. The messiah will be a lion, of the tribe of Judah and the root of David. He will be a warrior king like unto David, with the expectation that he will restore Israel and destroy Israel's enemies. As we read this, we are ready for the appearance of the lion.

And we see instead a lamb. A lamb! John now notes, standing near the throne is a lamb. And we are jarred to a stop. We are expecting a lion and we get a lamb? That is a staggering change in imagery. It feels like all our expectations are thrown off. I have to ask, Has God changed his mind?

And the answer is no, God hasn't changed. Let me share some thoughts on this lamb imagery:

- First and foremost, this change is not to be seen as a contradiction. This is not a denial of the Old Testament promises and expectations. Quite the contrary, in the wisdom of God, all the Old Testament promises and expectations for the lion are fulfilled in the Lamb!

- John's imagery here ought to make us think of Palm Sunday. The crowds on that first Palm Sunday came out to welcome the warrior king who was coming to throw off the Romans. They expected a warrior, with sword and shield, and riding a great warhorse. In anticipation of that, they lined the streets, threw their garments on the ground, waved palm branches, and shouted. But in actual fact they received Jesus. Jesus comes not on a warhorse but on a donkey, a symbol of humility and service. Jesus comes as a servant who will wash feet and bear a cross. He will not kill his enemies, He will, rather, die for the sake for his enemies. John's imagery here in Revelation is right in line with what Jesus did in his earthly ministry.

- Please note, and this is John's point, this Lamb, this Jesus of Palm Sunday, does conquer! This one who suffers and serves and dies does conquer the world and all that is opposed to God. All the promises for the lion, all the expectations for the messiah, are fulfilled in Jesus.

- This picture of Jesus as the Lamb opens up all sorts of associations for us. We have to start thinking of all that a lamb implies. We have to think of the exodus story back in the Old Testament, where the blood of a lamb saved the people and set them free. We have to think of the suffering servant proclaimed in Isa 53:7—"Yet he did not open his mouth; like a lamb that is led to the slaughter." We have to think of all sorts of associations like humility, accessibility, gentleness, care. This image of the Lamb helps us to see and understand who Jesus is.

- This is a good point to remind ourselves how John uses symbols. He doesn't use symbols to hide his message but to help us see his message. The lamb imagery isn't a code that is meant to disguise who Jesus is. Quite the contrary, the imagery of the Lamb is intended to open our imaginations to all sorts of associations and implications. The symbol helps us to get a better sense of who Jesus is and what He is doing. We do well to ask ourselves, what does it mean for our faith to confess that Jesus is the Lamb of God?

I was teaching a class on Revelation a while back. One of the members was a sweet elderly lady. We were talking about this lion and lamb imagery. She thought about it, then said, "I love this. When I'm in distress, I'm not going to go to a lion. But a lamb, that's what I need. It tells me that Jesus is accessible, caring, that He will welcome me. This image invites me to Jesus." I thought yes, you get it! That is exactly what John invites us to see.

The image of the Lamb now becomes the dominant symbol in Revelation for Jesus. As we read on in the next few verses (vv. 6–7), John shares more about this Lamb. The Lamb has been slaughtered—Jesus has died and rose again. The Lamb has seven horns. A horn in the book of Psalms was a symbol of royal power. Seven horns mean that Jesus has power, complete power. Jesus comes as a Lamb, yes, but make no mistake. He comes in the entire power of God! And Jesus has seven eyes—He is filled with God's Holy Spirit and knows what is going on in God's creation.

Notice, please, the Lamb does not replace God in John's imagery. The Lamb rather joins God at the throne and as the center of worship. The Lamb doesn't replace God. The Lamb rather is the means by which God works out his purpose of redemption. Revelation is clearly and loudly identifying Jesus as the Son of God, the one who shares in the very identity of God. Reading Revelation will always point us to the lordship of Jesus Christ!

Continuing on with chapter 5, Jesus takes the scroll from the hand of God. And the very cosmos erupts in worship! It is magnificent! The four living creatures, the elders, myriads of angels, all creation break forth into praise and song—"Worthy is the Lamb that was slaughtered to receive power and wealth and wisdom and might and honor and glory and blessing!" (v. 12). This language might sound familiar to you; we use it in many of our hymns and songs of praise, and we should! When we get a view of who Jesus is, the only fitting response is praise and thanksgiving. Revelation again reveals itself as a book of worship and perhaps it is in worship that we most fully appreciate what God is about.

Jesus is the Lamb, the Lamb of God. I suspect this message is just as radical in our modern world as it was to the first-century congregations listed in Revelation. I suspect we too have expectations that God will come in power and judgment to smite our enemies. We too think that "might makes right." We seek a warrior who sets up the kingdoms and institutions that we want. We do well to instead focus on this image of Jesus as the Lamb and what that means for us. We do well to reflect on the sheer grace of a God who died for his enemies, and yes who died for us. We do well to be moved by this Lord who serves and loves. And we do well to be directed by this Lord to be more and more of a people who serve and love. The way of the Lamb is the path of Christians right into eternity!

The lion is the Lamb. That is staggering! It is the way of God and the way of life!

QUESTIONS

1. Do you see Jesus as a lion or a lamb? What is your favorite image for Jesus?

2. What does calling Jesus "the Lamb" suggest to you? What does it mean to confess that Jesus is the Lamb of God?

3. Are you surprised by John's change of imagery for Jesus, from lion to lamb?

4. Revelation is clear—Jesus is the Lamb of God and as the Lamb He conquers. How does Jesus as the Lamb conquer?

5. Are you aware of images in church buildings or paintings or art or songs that proclaim Jesus as the Lamb? Share a few.

6. If Jesus walked a path of service and love, what does that say for how we live our faith?

Section 8

The Four Horsemen

ONE OF THE MOST vivid images in Revelation is the four horsemen in chapter 6. John envisions four riders on richly colored horses charging toward us, with destruction and death in their wake. The horsemen come as a conquering force with violence, economic threats, and death; they shake this creation to its very core. Even a quick reading of this leaves us with a sense of unease and fear. We aren't sure what is going on, but we instinctively know it can't be good!

Let's take a look at these horsemen, first asking what they said to John's initial audience, and then asking what they say to us. I think we will find a message that spans the centuries. The four horsemen are found in Rev 6:1–8:

> Then I saw the Lamb open one of the seven seals, and I heard one of the four living creatures call out, as with a voice of thunder, "Come!" I looked, and there was a white horse! Its rider had a bow; a crown was given to him, and he came out conquering and to conquer.
>
> When he opened the second seal, I heard the second living creature call out, "Come!" And out came another horse, bright red; its rider was permitted to take peace from the earth, so that people would slaughter one another; and he was given a great sword.

> When he opened the third seal, I heard the third living creature call out, "Come!" I looked, and there was a black horse! Its rider held a pair of scales in his hand, and I heard what seemed to be a voice in the midst of the four living creatures saying, "A quart of wheat for a day's pay, and three quarts of barley for a day's pay, but do not damage the olive oil and the wine!"
>
> When he opened the fourth seal, I heard the voice of the fourth living creature call out, "Come!" I looked and there was a pale green horse! Its rider's name was Death, and Hades followed with him; they were given authority over a fourth of the earth, to kill with sword, famine, and pestilence, and by the wild animals of the earth.

So, the four horsemen. John begins chapter 6 by announcing that Jesus the Lamb opens the seals on the scroll that Jesus has received from the hand of God. When the first seal is opened, a voice from heaven thunders "Come!" and in response a white horse comes charging. The rider is described as having a bow and a crown, and he came out "conquering and to conquer."

A mounted archer would make people in first-century Asia Minor think of the Parthians. The Parthian Empire was the next empire to the east of the Roman Empire. The Roman lands ran up to the Euphrates River; the Parthian Empire began on the other side. The Romans of the first century could not subdue the Parthians, although they had tried. The Parthians had developed a strategy of using mounted archers to attack their enemies. Their technique was unique to the ancient world and was overpowering. The Romans couldn't figure out how to deal with them. The Roman Empire lived with a fear of a Parthian invasion and that fear is tapped with the imagery of this first horseman.[1]

A second horseman comes charging as the second seal is opened. This horseman rides a horse of bright red. He carries "a great sword." This horseman takes "peace from the earth, so that people would slaughter one another." It is violence, horrible violence!

The third seal is opened. Again, a voice says "Come!" and a third horseman appears. The horse is black, and the rider holds a

---

1. Koester, *Revelation and the End*, 82–84.

pair of scales in his hand. A voice announces, "A quart of wheat for a day's pay, and three quarts of barley for a day's pay, but do not damage the olive oil and the wine!" The symbol here is of economic hardship and chaos on the earth. A denarius was a standard day's pay for a laborer. So, you work all day for a quart of wheat or three quarts of barely—about enough to feed your family for the day. You could survive but for how long? The imagery paints a portrait of economic troubles and turmoil. (By the way, the horseman is instructed not to harm the oil or wine. The staples of life are unbelievably expensive, but the luxury items aren't affected. Is it ever the case in this world of ours that the poor suffer but the rich do just fine?)

Finally, we come to the fourth horseman. This time a "pale green" horse comes (think in terms of a ghastly, sickly green!) and the rider is identified as Death. Death and Hades are now given authority to kill off a quarter of the earth's population.

What do we do with all of this? These are frightening, even repulsive, images. What in the world is John doing? (In what follows I'm borrowing insights from Dr. Craig Koester who provides a powerful way of understanding all of this.)[2]

I believe what John is doing here is deliberately shaking the sense of security of the Christians in first-century Asia Minor. Think for a moment of how this message would sound in the congregation at Laodicea. We've previously talked about Laodicea; they are the rich congregation. They were a rich church in a wealthy town. They were affluent and saw themselves as self-sufficient. Most likely they had made their peace with the ways of Rome and were content in their own security. In ancient history this period is called the Pax Romana; it was meant to be a time to depend on Rome for growth and protection. The Christians in Laodicea were content in that and didn't feel a lot of urgency in their need for Jesus.

Now John asks the question, Are you really that secure? Notice how each of the horsemen pricks away at the sense of security in Laodicea:

---

2. For a fuller development of all of this, please see Koester, *Revelation and the End*, 81–86.

The first horseman asks, Remember the Parthians, off to your east? They are hostile, and Rome can't stop them. If they invade, they are going to get to Laodicea long before they get to Rome.

The second horseman: How about violence in your community? Are there areas in town that you avoid? Are you really safe on your own streets?

The third horsemen: How about the economy? Is it steady? Can you support yourself and your family? How secure is your business? We know from history that the ancient economy had more ups and downs than our modern one. A drought or disaster would send everything into a tailspin. Can you really provide for your family?

The fourth horseman proclaims, Death! Even if you can escape all these other threats, death is still coming. There is no escaping that.

What John is doing is systematically pricking away at the sense of security of the Christians in Laodicea. They think they are safe and comfortable in their own means. John is warning, you aren't as secure as you think you are.

At this point, let's jump two thousand years and ask what John might be saying to us. We too try to find our security and comfort in ourselves. I suspect that we as twenty-first century Americans are more focused on ourselves than even the first-century Laodiceans. We like to think we are safe and self-sufficient. We tend not to see a lot of need for God and easily leave faith on the back burner.

John is asking us, Are you really that secure? He is warning us of the shallowness of what we too often try to build our lives on. The four horsemen strip away at our sense of security.

The first horseman asks, Are we really safe in America? For years we said we were. We have two oceans to protect us and a strong military. We see ourselves as safe. September 11, 2001, stripped all that away. We now know all too well the threat of terrorist attacks on our homeland—not to even mention Russia and nuclear missiles.

The second horseman: How about violence? Are you safe in your town? Drive-by shootings, senseless murders. My goodness, we live in a day when schools and churches get shot up. After the last wave of church shootings, I had members in the congregation I served as pastor tell me they were carrying concealed handguns on Sunday morning, just to be on the safe side. Somehow knowing that there were guns in the worship space, even if they were supposed to be there for our protection, didn't make me feel safe. What kind of a world is it where we don't feel safe sending our children to school or going to worship?

The third horseman: How about the economy? Are we really as prosperous as we think? As I write this, inflation is growing at the fastest rate in forty years. Food and gas costs are out of control. For a while my retirement plan looked pretty good, now I don't know. I know many people struggle much more than I do.

The fourth horseman proclaims death. Even if we can escape all the rest, we still face our own inevitable demise. How did the last funeral you went to make you feel?

What John is doing is pricking away at our sense of security. We think we can make a life without God. We too often try to leave God on the back burner of our affairs. John very pointedly asks, How is that working for you? When you think about it, look at how vulnerable you are. You want to build a life out of the things of this world? Well, good luck with that. If we are honest, there is nothing in the things of this world to stand on or build a life on. In fact, notice the question with which John ends chapter 6. Who can stand? Given all these threats, can anyone or anything stand in the security of this world?

What John is doing here is great preaching! Sinners that we are, we think we can build our lives without God. John very systematically shows us, there is no security in the things of this world. We are exposed in all of our vulnerability.

Just a quick note for what lies ahead in Revelation. In chapter 6 John is taking away all earthly security. But in chapter 7 (and we will explore this in detail in the next section) John will point us to a different and lasting security. In chapter 7 John will answer the question of who can stand by pointing to Jesus. It is Jesus who provides the security and hope for life. Who can stand? Those who are sealed in Jesus Christ! John shows us the lack of security in this world and then points us to God's own security in Jesus.

Again, this is great preaching that John is doing. These four horsemen, in all their power and threat, help us to see where life needs to be rooted. John directs us from this world to the living Lord.

One more point: people often ask the question of Revelation, who is this book addressed to? Some people want to see Revelation simply as a history book, which addressed its message to first-century citizens of Asia Minor. Others, especially in our day, see Revelation as a futuristic book, which will only be fulfilled in future events that are only hinted at now. I'm going to suggest a better reading of Revelation. That is, Revelation is the word of God. Given that, it speaks to all generations. Revelation certainly had a message for first-century Laodicea. It has a message for us today, and it will continue to speak until Jesus returns. That is the power of the word of God. You can't limit this message to one generation. God's word is a word of power that speaks every time it is proclaimed.

Who can stand? The four horsemen show us that there is finally nothing in this world to build a life on. But John isn't finished! He is also pointing us to the living Lord Jesus Christ. And there is the foundation now and for eternity!

QUESTIONS

1. What do you think of this interpretation of the four horsemen as threatening our sense of security? Is this a helpful way to understand Revelation?
2. How do the horsemen make you feel?
3. What most threatens you, what makes you most worried, in your life?
4. Where do you find your safety and security?
5. What might it mean to stand in Jesus?
6. Is Revelation a book for all generations?

Section 9

Sealed in Christ
Who Can Stand? Those Who Are Sealed in Jesus!

REVELATION IS A BOOK that moves. Sometimes it feels like a freight train, it just keeps pounding away as it comes toward us. I feel that when we go through chapter 6 into chapter 7. Chapter 6 is judgment and warning—the four horsemen, persecution, the entire cosmos upended. Revelation pounds away at our senses. John rips away and shows the futility of all earthly security. The terrifying question at the end of the chapter is, Who can stand? Given all that can happen to us, given all the threats and worries of life, can anything or anyone stand?

It is great and honest preaching that John is doing. We try so hard to make our lives and families secure—we try to build foundations on which we can stand. John, however, shows us what we already know deep in our hearts—there is nothing on earth that is permanent or dependable. All you need to do is go to the funeral of one you deeply love to know the truth of this. Nothing of this earth is safe, none of it will last. We are always closer than we realize to despair. The question at the end of chapter 6 haunts us—Who can stand?

But Revelation keeps on rolling. In chapter 7 John answers his own question—Who can stand? Those who are sealed in Christ (vv. 3–4)! There is good news beyond the brokenness of this world.

There is hope even in the most hopeless of times. In Jesus Christ God gives us the security the world cannot. In chapter 7, in fact in the whole book of Revelation, John proclaims that those who are sealed in the living Lord can stand! In Jesus Christ there is life, forgiveness, newness, hope. In Jesus Christ we can stand, now and for eternity.

Chapter 7 is a word of assurance, hope, celebration. Yes, there are trials and tribulations in this world, and at times life will seem overwhelming. But don't fear. As Jesus Himself said in the Gospel of John, "Take courage; I have conquered the world!" (16:33) There is something we can depend on, or better, someone we can depend on. In the risen Lord Jesus there is victory. John in chapter 7 of Revelation proclaims that those who are sealed in Jesus can stand no matter what.

It is quite the statement. The statement also raises more questions. What does it mean to be sealed in Christ? Am I included? How do I know if I'm sealed in Christ? Let's take a look at all this. (In what follows, I'm indebted to the work of Dr. Craig Koester.)[1]

In Revelation, to be sealed means to belong to Jesus. It is to find life in Christ. It is nothing more and nothing less than being Christian. John, who loves picturesque language, says we are sealed in Christ. The imagery proclaims that we find our lives in Jesus.

Let me go a bit deeper. Sealing means belonging to Jesus. It means being written to the account of Jesus, if I might use banking terms. It means being given life in Jesus as children of the living God. I personally love to understand this image of sealing in terms of promise. Jesus as the risen Lord makes promises to you, to me, to all of his people. To be sealed is to be the recipient of all these promises. Here are some of the promises in which we stand:

- Jesus promises to forgive our sins. All of our wrongs, mistakes, brokenness have been carried to a cross. The debt is paid, and we are free!
- Jesus promises to lead us into new life, godly life.
- He promises to make us part of a new family, God's church.

1. Koester, *Revelation and the End*, 88–89.

- He promises us his care, his presence, no matter what we face in life.
- He promises us his Holy Spirit to guide and fill our lives.
- He promises us eternal life in his presence.

All of this is caught up in being sealed. It is to belong to Jesus and share in his fullness of life.

All of this sounds good, wonderful. But it also raises another question. How do we know if we are sealed? How do we know that this is really for us? Revelation, along with the rest of the New Testament, answers that by saying—listen to God's word. God's word in Jesus Christ is that He loves you. God's promise to you is that you are invited into God's forgiveness and newness. It is God's gift, God's grace, for us. How do we know we are sealed? God in his word tells us so!

When we talk of being sealed in Christ, I think it is appropriate to hear echoes of baptism. John doesn't explicitly make this connection in Revelation, but Christians for centuries have spoken of baptism as being a sealing in Christ. Lutherans use this language in their baptismal service. When a baptism is performed, the pastor pours water over the person's head and says "I baptize you in the name of the Father and of the Son and of the Holy Spirit." Then the pastor makes the sign of the cross on the person's forehead and says "you have been sealed in the Holy Spirit and marked with the cross of Christ forever!" I can't help but think that John would happily add an "amen" to that.

To be sealed is to belong to Christ. That is the promise that undergirds all of life; it is the foundation and security for life now and eternally. Who can stand in the midst of all the trials of this world? Those who belong to Jesus!

Now to be clear, this is not a guarantee that Christians are exempt from the sufferings of this world. Quite the contrary, John warns Christians that they will suffer. This is not the promise of being exempt from suffering. But it is the promise of being held by Christ through all suffering. The Lord who suffered for us now walks with us and holds us in all that we deal with. We can depend on Him, and in Jesus we dare look forward to the new heaven and new earth where suffering is gone. In that we can stand!

It is quite the move that John is making. In chapter 6 he takes away all earthly security. In chapter 7 he gives ultimate security in Jesus. We stand, we live, in the power of the risen One!

Let me share an additional thought on this. When we talk about being sealed, don't get overly literal in this. (In all of Revelation, be careful not to be overly literal!) To be sealed does not mean that Christians have a cross literally engraved on their foreheads. This is rather language of promise, of orientation, of ownership. To be sealed is to belong to the Lord who has claimed you through the cross. It is not a physical marking but God's promise, a life-giving reality, as we find ourselves in Jesus. It is that promise that is foundational for all of life!

That's the point of all of this. John has shown in chapter 6 that there is no security in the ways of this world. As a good friend of mine used to say, the things of this world are finally dust and rust. But there is security and hope and freedom. It is found in God's gift of Jesus Christ. It is meant for you. We are sealed in the risen Lord.

QUESTIONS

1. Where do you find security for your life?
2. Does Jesus provide security for you?
3. Are you "sealed in Christ"? What does that language mean to you?
4. How do we know that we are sealed in Christ?
5. What do you think of the idea of baptism as being a sealing in Christ? Is baptism a promise for all of life?
6. Do any of these promises of Jesus particularly stand out for you?

Section 10

Faithful Witnessing

LET ME SHARE WITH you in one sentence what I believe is the message of Rev 11—*Christians are called to suffer persecution and even death for the faith, and God will use that suffering to reach out to a sinful world.* Wow. That is quite the statement. We are called to suffering and God will use that suffering? We need to explore that.

To begin, chapters 10 and 11 form a nice subunit in Revelation. Chapter 10 serves to introduce chapter 11; chapter 11 shares this powerful revealing of God's plan. Many students of Revelation have suggested that the message of chapter 11 is central for the book. In fact, to highlight that, John literally has placed chapter 11 at its center. Half of Revelation comes before chapter 11, half comes after. That spacing is one of the ways John highlights the centrality of what is said.

Chapter 11 tells us of two witnesses who speak to an unfaithful world (v. 3 and following). The two witnesses symbolize the church. (John refers to them in v. 4 as "lampstands," which he has told us in chapter 1 symbolize the church. Moreover the number two emphasizes the church's call to witness. In the Old Testament, two witnesses were required to guarantee the truth of what was said.)[1] These two witnesses speak God's word to the world and call

---

1. To further support this point that the two witnesses represent the church, G. B. Caird points out that the two witnesses in v. 3 are also described as "two

the world to repentance. (Verse 3 tells us the witnesses were "wearing sackcloth," a symbol of repentance.) The world doesn't listen; instead the world puts the two witnesses to death. In a further act of desecration, the bodies aren't even buried; they are left in the street (v. 8). In fact the world celebrates the death of the two witnesses (v. 10). God, however, raises the witnesses from the dead (v. 11). Amazingly, the world responds with many, many people coming to faith. Verse 13 tells us that 90 percent or nine-tenths of the people "gave glory to the God of heaven." A world that hasn't listened to God now overwhelmingly comes to faith.

What is going on here? Richard Bauckham, in his book *The Theology of the Book of Revelation*, provides a powerful reading of this. Revelation 11, Bauckham writes, calls for Christians/the church to bear witness to Jesus Christ. Christians will be persecuted and even put to death for this. But as the world sees the faithful witnessing of Christians, even unto death, people will be converted to Christ. In fact God will use this witness to call unbelievers to the life of faith. This faithful, suffering witnessing is the means that God will use to call unfaithful people back to Himself.[2]

It is quite the proclamation. Christians are called to faithful witness, even in a world that doesn't want to listen. Christians will suffer for this. But as the world sees this suffering witness, nonbelievers will realize the truth of the gospel and come to faith.

Again, that is quite the message. Yet if you think about it, this fits in perfectly with the words of Jesus. Jesus suffered and died to redeem the world and to call the world to faith. Jesus calls his followers to do the same. Jesus directs us in Matt 16:24 to "take up [our] cross and follow [Him]." Jesus calls for his followers to suffer for the faith. I don't think that is mere hyperbole on Jesus' part. I believe that is Jesus calling for Christians to faithfully follow Him, even to the point of death.

---

olive trees." John is drawing on imagery in Zech 4:14, where two olive trees refer to the anointed king and priest. John is again referring to the church: he has already told us in Rev 1:6, the church is "a kingdom, priests to God." For more on this, please see Caird, *Revelation*, 134.

2. Bauckham, *Theology of Revelation*, 80–88.

Take a moment and let this sink in. We are called to be faithful to Jesus in a world of sin and unbelief. The world will often oppose us, persecute us, even put us to death. God will use that persecution and opposition to win people for Himself. (It is no wonder that in chapter 10 of Revelation, John is told that this message is both "sweet and bitter." It is sweet; it involves the saving of many people. It is also bitter as it calls Christians to suffering.)

This is a challenging message, a sobering message. Suffering and persecution are part of what it means to follow Jesus. Christians in our day often don't think of the possibility of persecution, especially in the United States. We think we are beyond the years when that happened. But the Bible constantly foretells persecution and suffering for the faith as a reality for Christians, and we need to be aware of that. The fact is, persecution is a reality for many believers in our day. The twentieth century saw the death of more Christians for the faith than any previous century. I'm afraid that the twenty-first century will set a new record. Even in the United States, opposition to Christianity is on the rise. We more and more find ourselves in opposition to the ways of our culture, and I think that will and does result in persecution. Revelation is accurate in its focus on this.

Revelation 11 says that Christians will face suffering and opposition for the faith. Then John goes even further. He writes that as nonbelievers see Christians willing to suffer for the faith, the reality of the faith will come home to them. God will use the faithful witnessing of Christians in times of suffering to show the world the truth of the gospel. Through this witnessing unbelievers will come to faith.

It is quite the message. This is a powerful example of what Martin Luther called the "theology of the cross." Luther saw the cross as central for God's plan of redemption. Jesus redeemed us through his death on the cross, and we as Christians are called to "bear our cross," i.e., face suffering and death, as Christians. But it is precisely through all of this that God reaches and redeems a sinful humanity.[3]

3. Forde, *Where God Meets Man*, 33–44.

Revelation 11 says that Christians are called to suffer and even die for the sake of the faith, as God uses our witness to call nonbelievers to faith. My question becomes, Does this work? Does this really happen? I'm convinced that it does. Let me share with you three examples, one from history and two that I've seen.

First, an example from history: There was a famous early church theologian in the second century named Tertullian. He noted how as the Roman Empire persecuted Christians and put them to death, more and more people became Christians. Persecution and martyrdom didn't destroy the church; on the contrary the church grew as people saw the faithful witness of Christians. Thus, Tertullian famously taught that the blood of martyrs is the seed of the church.[4]

The second example is closer to our modern day. A number of years ago, I was doing chaplaincy work at the University of Kentucky Medical Center in Lexington. One evening when I was on duty, a young woman died after a long and hard struggle. She had suffered horribly, but she had been incredibly faithful and gracious in her witness to Jesus through it all. It wasn't easy for her, of course not. It had been hard, terrible, but she knew her Lord. I was in the room with the medical staff and family shortly after she passed. The doctors, the nurses, the family, and I stood around her still body on the bed. We joined hands. We cried and we prayed. God was so present in that room; it was one of the most powerful moments I've ever experienced in ministry. I am convinced that through her faithful witness I had a view straight into heaven that evening. Her suffering, faithful witness opened all of our eyes to God's presence.

My third example occurred a few years ago when I was teaching on Revelation in Ethiopia. I was in Dessie, in northern Ethiopia, teaching a group of around two hundred pastors and church leaders. The Mekane Yesus, a Lutheran denomination in Ethiopia, was at that time and still is one of the largest and fastest growing church bodies in the world. They literally struggle to keep up with all the growth as millions of people come to faith!

4. Tertullian, *Apology*, ch. 50 (*ANF* 3:108).

Faithful Witnessing

The church leaders and I worked our way through the book of Revelation, and in the process of our days together I listened to their stories. Most of the older pastors had served through the years of communist rule that Ethiopia suffered in 1974–87. The church was banned in those years, yet they persisted. Most of the older people in the room had been imprisoned, beaten, watched loved ones die, all for the sake of the faith. In addition I happened to be in Ethiopia at a time when Islamic terrorists were burning down Christian churches in the area. Many of the younger pastors had had their buildings burned, but they rebuilt, sometimes more than once, and continued to minister. I quickly realized that I was in a room filled with people who were much more profound in the faith than I was! These were people who had suffered for the faith and yet remained firm. I marveled how, in the midst of all of that opposition and suffering, the church in Ethiopia grew astronomically.

We worked our way through Revelation and came to chapter 11. I explained to them what I've written here, that chapter 11 calls for Christians to be faithful in the midst of suffering and persecutions, and God uses that suffering to reach out to nonbelievers. Then I asked the people, does this plan work? I told them to connect their experiences of persecution with the promises of chapter 11, and I suggested to them that God was doing just as He said. Their faithful witness was used by God to grow God's church. They began nodding in agreement as they saw the truth of what Revelation proclaimed. They had indeed lived out the promises of chapter 11.

God has a plan, and as chapter 10 says, it is bittersweet. Christians are called to faithful witnessing in a hostile world. The world will oppose us, even persecute us. But we bear witness nonetheless. And through our witness God leads people to Himself. That is the call, the challenge, the privilege, of being Christian.

QUESTIONS

1. Do you think that our culture is moving in a more "non-Christian" direction? What makes you think that?

2. Have you ever faced opposition or hostility for being Christian?

3. How do you react to this message in chapter 11 of Revelation? Is it indeed the case that Christians will suffer persecution and opposition, but God uses their witness to win others for Christ?

4. What might "bearing the cross" look like in our modern culture?

5. Is this message of chapter 11 "bitter and sweet"? How so?

6. Share an example of a faithful witness that you have seen.

Section 11

Judgment in Revelation

ONE OF THE TOPICS for which Revelation is known is judgment. Even people who aren't familiar with the book know that there is a lot of judgment and warning in its pages. Revelation is associated with destruction, wrath, plagues, etc.

I certainly agree; it is the case that there is a good deal of judgment in the book. I have been arguing that Revelation is more about promise than judgment, and I believe that. But that doesn't mean that judgment isn't a strong presence in the book. It is obviously part of John's writing, and some of the most graphic and harshest words of judgment in the Bible are found in Revelation. You can't deal with Revelation and not deal with judgment. And so our question for this section becomes, What do we do with these images of judgment? How do we read them? How do we hear them? Or perhaps a better question, What is God telling us in these images?

It is fascinating to me, we live in a time and age when people don't want to hear of judgment. We don't want to talk of the judgment of God; in fact in our modern day we too often go to the extreme of thinking that God wouldn't do such a thing. I fear that there is a move in the modern church to want to see God as a kind of a supernatural Santa Claus, loving to be sure but never judging. We don't talk about God as one who would challenge us or correct us or oppose the wrongs that we do. We want to block out any words of judgment, particularly by God.

Revelation won't let us go that route. There is judgment, strong words of judgment, in Revelation, and we have to hear that. To expand the scope, this theme of judgment doesn't just occur in Revelation; it occurs throughout the Bible. God, in the Scriptures, is most certainly shown to be the God of love, the creator and redeemer whose steadfast love endures forever. But the Bible also proclaims that God detests sin, opposes injustice, and is at work against destruction and greed. Judgment is a powerful and vital theme in the Bible. Faithful Christians, and particularly faithful readers of Revelation, need to deal with all of that.

There are words of judgment in Revelation: powerful, overwhelming words and images. To list only a few—Death and Hades given authority over a quarter of the earth (6:7–8), the sun turning black and stars falling to the earth (6:12–13), grotesque locust-like creatures ravaging and attacking people (9:1–11), horrifying hordes of mounted cavalry with horses spewing smoke and sulfur that kill scores of people (9:13–19), a burning and smoldering lake of fire for Satan and his cohorts (19:20 and 20:10). There is all sorts of destruction and havoc and judgment in this book.

What do we do with all this language and these images? Some readers of Revelation take all this imagery and try to construct some future time line of horror and devastation. They try to map out a future of plagues and destruction. I don't find that helpful or appropriate. In the first place, Revelation isn't written to give us a detailed road map to the future. Revelation just isn't written for that. Second, that approach really doesn't wrestle with what John is doing with the words of judgment. John is a profound preacher and theologian. He is telling us things about the nature of our world and about the reality of our God. We need to dive deeply into the words of Revelation and explore and wrestle with what John is saying with all these images.

So, let's take a look at judgment in the book of Revelation. To begin, let me share a reminder about the book. Revelation is symbolic literature. The power of the book is in its use of symbols to proclaim its message. As we have said repeatedly, don't take the symbols literally. Rather ask, What are the symbols saying? The symbols in Revelation work to engage us, to involve our minds and imaginations and help us to see more into the nature and ways of this world and of our Lord. Don't take the symbols literally, rather ask how they function.

Let me give you an example of this, an example that I've used before. John in Revelation loves to refer to Jesus as "the Lamb." That is John's favorite and most frequently used symbol for Jesus and it is powerful. Please don't take the symbol literally—John is not saying that Jesus has hooves or wool! John rather uses the symbol of the Lamb to help us see things about Jesus. Referring to Jesus as the Lamb opens up all sorts of associations for who Jesus is—sacrificial, giving, the Passover lamb, the suffering servant in Isa 53, gentle, accessible. The symbol helps us to see who Jesus is. We are not to take the symbol literally. We rather ask, What is John saying by use of this symbol?

That is the case with words of judgment also. These words also are symbols. We ought not to take them literally as if we will try to graph out future horrors for this planet. We rather ask, How do these symbols function? What is John telling us with these words of judgment?

Let me share three insights into what I see John doing. First, these words of judgment function as words of warning. John uses language of judgment to warn his original readers, and us, to avoid the sins and evils of this world.

Think about that. The scenes of judgment function as words of warning. John uses graphic and harsh language to steer us away from that which is evil. John is not simply laying out predictions of horror to come; he is warning us, in the here and now of our lives, to steer away from that which is destructive to life.

Let me share an example of this in Revelation. In chapters 16, 17, and 18, John writes in graphic symbols of judgment that will befall Rome. One of his points in doing so is to warn Christians not to accept the ways of Rome. John saw the Roman Empire as rooted in evil; as such he warns the Christians against accommodating themselves to Roman ways.

It is helpful for me to read the judgments of chapters 16, 17, and 18 in light of previous words that John has shared in chapter 2. In 2:12–17, John warns the Christians in Pergamum not to accept Roman ways. John is well aware that one of the temptations for the Christians in Pergamum was to accommodate to the ways of Roman culture. The Christians were considering eating meat offered to idols, worshiping Roman gods, sharing in Rome's vision of empire. In chapter 2 John warns the Christians that Rome is evil and Christians must not accommodate themselves to Rome.

In chapters 16, 17, and 18, John repeats this warning, only now in more graphic and horrific terms. He writes of judgment that will befall Rome. And his not-so-subtle question is—Christians, do you really want to accommodate yourselves to that which will be destroyed and judged?

The words of judgment function as words of warning. I would add, this is also often the case in Scripture as a whole. Words of judgment and destruction warn us from evil. We are reminded in stark and graphic terms to steer clear of that which is ultimately evil and life-destroying.

Words of judgment in Revelation function as words of warning. By the way, this also helps us to understand some of the extremely harsh images of Revelation. The harsher images function as louder words of warning. The harsh images grab our attention and show us that things are wrong.

Let me give you a different sort of example of how this works. Our family home is on a large lake. We have a canoe on our lakeshore. When my children were young, they enjoyed taking the canoe out on the lake. I was always clear with them: stay close to shore in the canoe. Our lake can get rough quickly; winds and waves can appear that will swamp a canoe. The further out you go in the water, the more dangerous it can be. My instructions, usually given in calm language, were to stay close to shore.

I remember one afternoon, my children were in the canoe and getting far from shore. I could see a storm coming. I was worried. I stood on the shore and yelled at them to come in. They couldn't, or wouldn't, hear me. I got louder and louder and I'm sure my voice sounded harsher and harsher, not because I was being vengeful on my children but because I had to get their attention and call them back to safety. Some of my neighbors might have wondered why I was yelling so harshly at my children, but I had to get their attention. My aim was to warn them of danger that was all too close.

I believe that the graphic scenes of judgment in Revelation function in the same way. The Christians that Revelation was originally addressed to were in danger of following Rome into destructive practices. The glory of Rome had blinded some Christians to the dangers of Rome. John yells words of warning at them to get their attention and to call them back to the safety of obedience. The words of judgment function as warning.

To go further with this, we as modern readers of Revelation need to be aware of this. Revelation should call us to discern and avoid the evils of our day. The danger of accommodating to the ways of the world wasn't just a first-century danger. It is still a very real temptation in our modern day. We live in a society that calls to us with materialism, sexual exploitation, self-centeredness, and greed. One of the vital messages of Revelation for our modern day is to warn us away from all that isn't of God. We need to see our world with John's discerning eye and hear and heed warnings against the seductiveness of the sins of our day.

That's first: the words of judgment in Revelation function as words of warning. Second, an additional thought on judgment in Revelation: it serves the goal of liberation. Judgment isn't about getting even; it serves the greater goal of liberation and new life.

In Revelation, evil will be judged. Why? In order to set free those enslaved by evil. As evil is stopped, people are freed to new life and hope.

It is worth noting, many of the images of judgment in Revelation are taken from the Old Testament exodus story. (For examples, see Exod 8:7, 8–9, 12; 9:1–11; 16:2–4, 10–11.) In the book of Exodus, the people of Israel are slaves in Egypt. God determines to set the people free. Pharaoh, the ruler of the Egyptians, opposes

God and won't free the people. There is a series of plagues that finally overwhelm Pharoah, and he lets the people of Israel go. In Exodus, the plagues/judgment serve the goal of liberation.

Many of the scenes of judgment in Revelation are drawn from and rooted in the plagues of the exodus story. John wants us to think of the exodus story as we are reading all of this. John particularly wants us to remember one of the themes from the exodus story—judgment serves the cause of liberation.

For a particularly powerful example of this, let me refer again to chapters 16, 17, and 18 of Revelation. As we noted, these chapters contain graphic and harsh scenes of judgment. The language is horrifying, provocative, overwhelming, as the evil of the world, and particularly the evils of Rome, are judged. (In fact, much of the imagery in chapter 16 is taken from the exodus story.) Chapters 16, 17, and 18 portray judgment on the evils of this earth. Then in chapter 19 the scene shifts from earth to heaven. In heaven there is rejoicing and celebration (19:1–5). Heaven celebrates because the evil on earth has been stopped and God's servants and God's creation are freed. Chapter 19 sounds like Handel's "Hallelujah" chorus, and in fact the "Hallelujah" chorus is based on this passage.[1] The very heavens ring with the song of liberation and deliverance. The judgment served the goal of liberation.

When we read words of judgments in Revelation, we do well to keep in mind this overarching theme. Judgment serves the cause of liberation, as God works to bring in his new creation of freedom and grace.

Third, a final thought on judgment in Revelation, and this is closely related to what has just been shared: There is a powerful phrase in Rev 11:18 for understanding how judgment functions. Judgment in Revelation is about "destroying those who destroy the earth."

I find that phrase most helpful in understanding judgment. In the book, John points out repeatedly that evil is given every opportunity to repent. That which is evil is time and again called to repentance. But when evil won't change, it must ultimately be

---

1. Koester, *Revelation and the End*, 35–36.

destroyed as God brings about his new creation. Unrestrained evil will continue to destroy the world. God won't let that happen. That which insists on being destructive must be stopped.

I think that sometimes Christians mistakenly work with what I call a "lifeboat" theory of salvation. What I mean by this is that we understand that God created a good earth and that sin now mars God's good creation. We see salvation as God rescuing those who believe in Him from the evils of the earth. Salvation is like a lifeboat where believers are rescued but the rest of creation continues to sink in sin and destruction.

To John's mind, that isn't enough. God certainly rescues all who call upon Him. But God is also out to reclaim his creation. God isn't content to leave evil in control. The earth is the Lord's and the Lord will make it new. Anything evil, anything that stands in the way of God's new creation is given all sorts of opportunities to repent. If it finally won't change it must be stopped as God brings in his newness. All that destroys the earth—hatred, prejudice, violence, bigotry, greed—must be stopped to make way for the new creation.

John has a powerful and all-encompassing vision of salvation. God rescues individual people, of course. God will also rescue the entire creation. John's vision is clear, God's victory in Jesus Christ is cosmic in its reach and an entire new heaven and new earth are a-coming!

Judgment in Revelation: It is a powerful component of the book. It is language that makes us uncomfortable and that we need to wrestle with. But it is language we need to hear as we follow this God who indeed makes all things new!

QUESTIONS

1. Do you see a lot of judgment in the book of Revelation? Is that worrisome to you?
2. Will God judge evil?

3. How do you understand/deal with the words of judgment in Revelation?

4. Does judgment in Revelation (and the Bible) serve the goal of liberation? How so?

5. Will God "destroy the destroyers of the earth"? What might that mean?

6. Do you agree that God's ultimate goal is redemption and new life?

Section 12

Rapture or Not!

"So, what does Revelation teach about the rapture?" That is a question that has come up in every class I've ever taught on Revelation, as some people associate Revelation with a rapture. The question always comes up and always sparks some interesting and often intense discussion. Inevitably in classes there are Christians who have never heard of this thing called the rapture and aren't sure what the word refers to. There are other Christians who are convinced that the rapture will be God's next great activity in the history of this world and we better be ready for it. It seems like everyone wants to know what Revelation says.

So, let's look at this idea of a rapture. Let me explain what it is and where it comes from. Then let's look at what Revelation actually says. Let me be clear from the outset, as I study the Bible and especially Revelation, I don't believe that the Bible teaches that there will be an event called the rapture. It just isn't what John and the rest of the New Testament writers are teaching.

Before getting to the theory of a rapture, let me begin with a doctrine of Christian theology that the Bible and all Christians do affirm—that is, that Jesus will come again. Let me be very clear on this. Jesus has promised, and the Scripture is clear, Christ will come again. We often refer to this as the second coming. At some future point Christ will return in all his glory. With his coming, human history will end and He will establish the fullness of God's kingdom. That is a vital promise that Jesus made back in his earthly ministry and that the church has lived with for centuries. Revelation and the entire New Testament are clear that Christ will come again.

But here is where the idea of a rapture clouds the picture. The rapture is a teaching that says seven years before Christ's return, an event called the rapture will occur. The teaching is that in a blink of an eye, all true believing Christians will be taken from the earth and lifted to heaven. That event is called the rapture. This teaching believes that affairs on this earth will get worse and worse; when things are too bad, God will miraculously "rapture" or rescue all believers and bring them to heaven. When the rapture occurs, cars will literally be without drivers, planes without pilots, families at home will suddenly be missing their believing members. All true believers will be instantaneously taken to heaven; all nonbelievers will be left behind here on the earth. Following this rapture there will be seven years of absolute terror and evil on earth. At the end of this seven years, Jesus will then return and vanquish all evil.

So again, all Christians believe in what we call the second coming, that Jesus will return in glory. The rapture enthusiasts add to that and say that seven years before Jesus' return an event called the rapture will remove all true Christians from earth. Interestingly, this idea of a rapture is a relatively recent idea. It actually begins in the mid-1800s with the writings of a clergyman in England named John Nelson Darby. For the first 1,800 years of the church's life, there is no mention of a rapture or reference to it. The idea begins with Darby; his study of Scripture led him to develop the idea of a rapture and a whole theological system around it. (That system is usually referred to as "premillennial dispensationalism.") Darby's teachings didn't take much root in England but were brought to the United States in the latter part of the nineteenth century.[1] They took root in the United States and have been fairly popular ever since. Popular writings about the rapture include the *Scofield*

---

1. Koester, *Revelation and the End*, 19–26.

Reference Bible of 1909, *The Late Great Planet Earth* by Hal Lindsey in the 1970s, and the Left Behind series in the early twenty-first century. All of these writings have been runaway bestsellers.

Given this idea of a rapture, the next question for us to ask is, What does the Bible have to say about this? Since this study is focusing on Revelation, let me add, What does Revelation in particular say about a rapture? The answer is, Revelation does not speak of a rapture. The word "rapture" does not occur in Revelation (nor in the rest of the Bible!). The concept of a rapture is not to be found in Revelation; moreover I fear that the idea of a rapture actually contradicts what Revelation does teach. Revelation just does not teach that there will be an event called the rapture.

Proponents of a rapture will argue that the idea of a rapture is to be found both in Revelation and throughout the Bible. They argue that when John is given his heavenly vision in Rev 4, that is actually a rapture or rapture foreshadowing event. I don't find that persuasive. We have to note that John doesn't see chapter 4 as a rapture event. John understands himself as recording a visionary experience he had, an experience similar to experiences that Paul mentions in 2 Cor 12 and that Peter shares in Acts 10. Chapter 4 in Revelation records a visionary experience given to John, not a rapture of the church.

The rapture proponents will also argue that from chapters 4 through 19 in Revelation the Greek word for church—namely, *ecclesia*—is not used by John. (Revelation was originally written in Greek.) Moreover, they argue the church is not mentioned on earth in these chapters because the church has been raptured. Again I find that to be a strange interpretation of Revelation. It is the case that John doesn't use the word *ecclesia* in chapters 4–19, but he makes all sorts of references to the church. John is a profound writer and artist; he uses colorful images to refer to the church. For example, in chapter 11 two witnesses are described in terms that tell us they represent the church in its call to witness here on earth. In chapter 12 the church—"those who keep the commandments of God and hold to the testimony of Jesus" (12:17)—is clearly on the earth and being persecuted by Satan. This list could go on. There are a host of images in Rev 4–19 that refer to the church here on the earth. Christians have not nor will they be raptured; the idea of a rapture simply is not to be found in Revelation. This idea of a rapture has to be read into the book, and that is a dangerous way to approach the Scriptures.

The proponents of a rapture will argue that the clearest biblical reference to a rapture is found in 1 Thess 4:15–18. Since that passage is lifted up quite a bit, and is often accepted as a "proof text" for a rapture, let's look at it here:

> For this we declare to you by the word of the Lord, that we who are alive, who are left until the coming of the Lord, will by no means precede those who have died. For the Lord himself, with a cry of command, with the archangel's call and with the sound of God's trumpet, will descend from heaven, and the dead in Christ will rise first. Then we who are alive, who are left, will be caught up in the clouds together with them to meet the Lord in the air; and so we will be with the Lord forever. Therefore encourage one another with these words.

At first glance this seems to be a reference to the rapture. Christians caught up in the air to meet Jesus, isn't that the rapture? The answer is no, and to see why we need to look at the whole passage of what Paul writes. Let me add the two verses that precede what was just shared, as they explain what Paul is referring to:

> But we do not want you to be uninformed, brothers and sisters, about those who have died, so that you may not grieve as others do who have no hope. For since we believe that Jesus died and rose again, even so, through Jesus, God will bring with him those who have died. For this we declare to you by the word of the Lord, that we who are alive, who are left until the coming of the Lord, will by no means precede those who have died. For the Lord himself, with a cry of command, with the archangel's call and with the sound of God's trumpet, will descend from heaven, and the dead in Christ will rise first. Then we who are alive, who are left, will be caught up in the clouds together with them to meet the Lord in the

air; and so we will be with the Lord forever. Therefore encourage one another with these words. (4:13–18)

First Thessalonians was one of the earliest letters that Paul wrote, probably within twenty years or so of Jesus' resurrection. In the letter Paul addresses a number of concerns that the people in Thessalonica have raised, including one in particular in chapter 4. The Christians are awaiting the second coming of Jesus and they expect it to happen in the near future. But some of the Christians have died in the time before Christ has returned. The Thessalonians are worried: Will those who have died in Christ be included in the resurrection when Christ returns?

Paul writes this beautiful passage in chapter 4 to answer that question. What Paul is proclaiming is of course they will! In fact Paul proclaims that "the dead in Christ will rise first," they will be at the front of the resurrection. The passage is actually a pastoral answer from Paul. Christians need not worry about the salvation of deceased loved ones. It is an explanation of what will happen at the second coming of Jesus, as well as words of assurance from Paul.

When you read the entirety of this 1 Thessalonians passage, it becomes quite clear that this isn't a reference to a rapture. We need to constantly dig deeply into Scripture and wrestle with what it says![2]

I don't believe the Bible teaches there will be a rapture. Let me go one step further: I also believe this rapture teaching obscures and confuses what the call to discipleship actually is for Christians. Let me explain. The rapture theory basically says that when things get bad enough, God will take the true believers out of the earth. They won't face suffering as God rescues them to heaven. It is an appealing and basically triumphalist theology.

That is just the opposite of what Revelation teaches. Revelation does warn us of suffering and trials ahead. But rather than

---

2. If you would like to read more critiques of this idea of a rapture, let me suggest two books. The first is a book by Barbara Rossing entitled *The Rapture Exposed*. This is a thorough critique of why the idea of a rapture just isn't biblical. In addition, the second edition of my book *Come, Lord Jesus* contains an appendix that lays out and critiques the idea of a rapture.

escaping the trials, Christians are called to be faithful to Christ in the midst of trials. Christians aren't to escape trials but rather be faithful through the trials. By their faithfulness, especially in persecution and even death, the Christians give witness to the victory of Jesus Christ.

Think about that for a moment. Isn't that the path that Jesus took? Jesus went through the persecution and trial of the cross. God didn't miraculously rescue Jesus from the cross; the true miracle is that God let his Son die for our sake. Jesus was faithful in the midst of suffering and through that worked our redemption. Now Jesus bids us to be willing to bear the cross; that is clear throughout the New Testament and particularly in Revelation. We are called to be faithful in the midst of a world that is so often opposed to God. That will lead to sufferings and challenges for Christians; and John calls for us to be faithful witnesses in the midst of that. Revelation isn't about escaping the world but rather living faithfully in the midst of this world. I believe that what John is doing in Revelation is lifting up this "theology of the cross" and calling for Christians to be faithful even and especially in the midst of suffering and persecution. John goes so far as to point out that through that faithful witness the world will see the truth of Jesus.[3]

For these and other reasons, I don't believe in the idea of a rapture. Let me also note, there are many devout Christians in our day who do believe that a rapture will occur. We need to be respectful of them and perhaps help them to look at Revelation in a new way. The most helpful approach to dealing with this, and with all questions of what Christians believe, is to engage in a deep, deep study of Scripture and wrestle with what the Bible actually says. There can be no substitute for an ongoing study of God's word!

So, with all this said, what does Revelation teach? Let me summarize and notice how beautifully Revelation fits in with the rest of the New Testament. Revelation teaches that Jesus Christ has entered this world of sin and hurt. Jesus is the one who was faithful

---

3. For a powerful laying out of this, please see Bauckham, *Theology of Revelation*, ch. 4. Bauckham does a masterful job of examining all of this, in Rev 10 and 11, in particular, but also in the whole book of Revelation.

unto death, dying on a cross for us. Through the cross God's victory has been won. But for now evil continues on this earth until the second coming of Christ.

As we live in this period between Jesus' resurrection and the second coming, we are called to be faithful witnesses to Jesus. We will deal with the evils and sufferings of this world; in fact, as we are faithful we can expect the opposition of the world. Sometime in the future, at a time known only by God, Jesus will return and bring in the fullness of God's kingdom. All evil will be destroyed; the "new Jerusalem," the city of God, will become the dwelling place of God and God's people. We look forward in hope to this new heaven and earth. In the meanwhile we live in the grace and care of our Lord now and we pray "Come, Lord Jesus" as we look to God's future.

QUESTIONS

1. Have you ever heard of the term "rapture"? Are you familiar with this teaching?
2. After reading this, do you think there will be a rapture? Why or why not?
3. Jesus will come again. That is one of the great promises of the Bible. What do you think this second coming of Christ will be like?
4. Revelation, and the Bible as a whole, teach that there will be sufferings and persecutions for those who are faithful in this world. We do not escape the sufferings of this world, but rather are called to be faithful to Jesus even in the sufferings of this world. How might this understanding shape your faith?
5. Does the prayer "Come, Lord Jesus" give you hope?

Section 13

666

I THINK IT SAFE to say that the best-known number in the book of Revelation is 666. Very often we aren't totally clear what it means, but we know it stands for evil. I think it is also safe to say that the number 666 has been used to create more mischief and havoc than any other number in the Bible. There is a long history of people labeling their opponents with the number 666 to discredit them. It is a number with a long and often inglorious history.

So what is 666? Let's do some digging. The number is found only once in Revelation, at the end of 13:18. The reading says: "This calls for wisdom: let anyone with understanding calculate the number of the beast, for it is the number of a person. Its number is six hundred and sixty-six." By way of background, John has introduced the concept of "the beast" in the first half of chapter 13. The beast is John's predominant image for speaking of the Roman Empire. The language is part of John's work to unveil or reveal to his readers what the Roman Empire really is. (Other images include a drunken prostitute in chapter 17!) Rome presents itself as the hope and salvation of the world. John scoffs at that and says no, the Roman Empire is better understood as a beast. It oversteps, devours, and destroys human life. John in chapter 13 is warning Christians not to accept the ways of Rome, for Rome is a beast rooted in the very power of Satan.

666

So far, so good—John says that Rome is a beast. But then he goes on to add that the beast has "a number," and the number is 666. How do we understand this? The number 666 is a symbol, and a symbol that functions at a couple of levels. (John loves symbols that can function in a number of ways, and that is the case here.) For the first level, 666 is a number that falls short of 777. Seven is a number of completeness or perfection in Revelation. (Notice all the sevens in the book of Revelation—seven churches, seven seals, seven spirits before the throne of God, seven trumpets, seven bowls of wrath, and on and on!) Seven in Revelation, and in the ancient world in general, was understood as a number that represented perfection. Seven repeated three times, or 777, would be a number of absolute perfection. Thus, 666 is that which falls short. "Close, but not quite," we might say in our modern jargon. John is warning Christians to beware of that which looks brilliant and great but which is ultimately flawed and evil. John is specifically thinking of the Roman Empire. The empire looks glorious; it presents itself as glorious. But John is saying at its core it is evil. The Roman Empire falls short of the glory it proclaims, and the Christians are warned to beware of the ways of Rome.

By the way, human history knows of too many of these things that present themselves as great but ultimately fall short into evil. For some twentieth century examples, how about Hitler and Nazi Germany? There was pride and power there, but as World War II painfully revealed, it was all ultimately evil. Or perhaps Stalin and the communist rule in the Soviet Union? John is warning, beware of that which says it is good and powerful but finally falls short, as it is corrupt and evil.

Let me push this a little further. Darrell Johnson, who wrote a book on Revelation entitled *Discipleship on the Edge*, coined a phrase that I find both memorable and helpful in understanding this impact of 666. Johnson writes that in the symbolism of Revelation, 666 is "completely incomplete."[1] As we have said, six is a number of incompleteness, that which falls short of seven. Three in Revelation and the New Testament is a number of completeness.

---

1. Johnson, *Discipleship*, 249.

(Think in terms of the Trinity!) Putting three sixes together gives us the strange combination of the completeness of incompleteness.

And yet when you think about it, isn't human history full of incomplete leaders or political parties or ideologies that demanded complete and ultimate allegiance? Again for obvious examples, think of Hitler and the Nazis or the Roman Empire. They portrayed themselves as the embodiment of power; they demanded complete allegiance. But as history has revealed, they were so incomplete, so evil. John, with the symbol 666, is saying beware of anything human (including political parties, ideologies, nationalism, human leaders), no matter how impressive or glorious, that demand complete or ultimate allegiance. For complete, ultimate allegiance must be reserved for God.

That is the first level at which 666 functions. But there is a second level to all of this. The symbol 666 is also rooted in the ancient practice of what is called gematria. In our modern day, numbers and letters are separate. We have our "1, 2, 3s" and our "A, B, Cs." In the ancient world, numbers and letters were one and the same. That was true for the Latin the Romans used. That meant that every number was a letter and every letter a number. It follows then that every name of a person had a numerical equivalent. You could add up the letters of a name and calculate the number of that name. For example, think of the name "Ada." A would be 1, D, 4, and the second A, again, 1. The number of Ada would be 6. Every name had a number.

Now in gematria, going from the name to the number is relatively simple. Going from the number back to the name is much more complicated. Our question for Rev 13:18 is, What name adds up to 666?

There are a number of possibilities and theories. But most biblical scholars believe 666 points to Nero, the Roman Emperor from AD 54–68. "Neron Kaiser" (or "Neron Caesar") in Hebrew characters adds up to 666.[2]

---

2. For a more complete explanation of this, please see Koester, *Revelation and the End*, 133. Dr. Koester does a masterful job of explaining all the numerical values here. One more point on this: gematria also explains a variant

666

The symbol 666 is meant to get the Christians thinking of the reign of Nero. Nero was the first Roman emperor to persecute Christians. Nero had Christians covered in animal skins and thrown to dogs, he crucified Christians, and he burned them to death. One of John's purposes in chapter 13 is to reveal the Roman Empire as a beast. By referring to Nero, John is laying that out very clearly for the Christians.

Identifying 666 with Nero also fits in with some earlier references in chapter 13. In 13:3 John writes about the beast and says, "One of its heads seemed to have received a death-blow, but its mortal wound had been healed." That is a not-so-subtle reference to Nero and later legends about Nero. Nero committed suicide in AD 68, but we know from Roman history that there were rumors in the empire that Nero didn't really die and that he would return. "A mortal wound that had been healed" is a reference to this legend. John in 13:3 has drawn a connection between the Roman Empire and the reign of Nero, and now in 13:18 with 666, he reinforces his point.

Given all of this, what John is saying in this passage is, Christians, beware of the ways of Rome. John uses the symbol of 666 to "unmask" Rome and say that Rome is a beast that looks a lot like Nero. Remember what Nero did, John is saying, and don't make your peace with the ways of the Roman Empire.

So, with all this said, are we done? Can we identify 666 with Nero and Rome and leave it at that? I think there is one more important move to make: that is to pick up what John is doing and carry that into our modern day. Following John's example, we do well to ask the question, Are there beasts in our modern world that need to be unmasked?

Think about that for a moment. I believe that Satan is still active in this world. He will be active until Jesus returns. Doesn't it make sense to assume that Satan is still raising up "beasts" to do his

---

reading of this verse. Check your Bible and see if it has a footnote after v. 18. Many translations do and the footnote says, "Some manuscripts read 616." Some ancient manuscripts of Revelation have 616 instead of 666. The spelling "Nero Kaiser" would add up to 616.

work? We as modern-day Christians don't need to beware of the Roman Empire. But if Satan is active, are there modern-day beasts that we need to beware of?

Adela Yarbro Collins writes, "The job of the Church in every age is to name the beast."[3] I love that quote. The job of the Church in every age is to name what is "beastly" at that time in history. As John teaches, when Satan raises up a beast, the beast will always disguise itself as good. The job of the church is to "name the beast," to point out evil for what it is. That is exactly what John did, and it is what we are called to do.

A great question from Rev 13 is, Are there beasts to be named in our day? Think about that, and let me suggest a few.

For one obvious beast, I'm going to suggest the Russian leader, Vladimir Putin. As I'm writing this, bombs and missiles are trying to destroy Ukraine. Putin has unleashed an all-out offensive that is destroying the country and killing all sorts of people including civilians. The images on the news each night are horrifying. Putin's claim is that the invasion is good and just. He says it is to liberate and denazify Ukraine. I think it is a beastly work and must be named for what it is.

For a second possibility, and this may be more controversial, but how about Hollywood? The entertainment industry certainly makes itself look good. It is glamorous, rich, flamboyant; the entire world watches Hollywood. And yet so many of the values are toxic—sex, exploitation, money, drugs. It seems to me that much of Hollywood is "beastly."

For another possibility, how about materialism? Jesus very clearly says that Christians cannot serve God and wealth. Many Christians, however, are willing to try. We live in a materialistic day that focuses on wealth and prestige and fulfilling our own wants. We need to critique those values in light of the Scripture. Perhaps our materialism is a modern-day beast.

Revelation gives us the tools to understand and speak to the evils of our day. It truly is the job of the church in every generation to "name the beast." As John wrote, this calls for wisdom, and I

---

3. Collins, *Crisis and Catharsis*, 175.

would add faith. Like John we need to be bold in our witness and discernment.

The number 666 is famous because of Revelation. John used it to warn of the dangers of the Roman Empire. We do well to be guided by John as we face the evils of our day.

QUESTIONS

1. Have you previously heard of the number 666? Have you heard of 666 being identified with a person, and if so who? What is your impression of 666?
2. Does identifying 666 in Revelation with Nero make sense to you?
3. We've suggested that John used 666 to "unmask" Rome, to show Rome for the evil that it was. Do you agree with that? Why or why not?
4. Have you seen modern examples of something evil that tries to make itself look good? Please share an example.
5. Are there "beasts" that should be named in our modern day? Think about what might be "beastly" in our world.

Section 14

Pick a Side

HAVE YOU EVER WATCHED a ping-pong game? The ball goes back and forth, back and forth. When I read Rev 12–14, I feel like I'm watching a ping-pong game. John keeps going back and forth between good and evil. He shows us evil, then he shows us good; he shows us evil and he shows us good. John challenges us in the midst of all that to pick one side or the other.

Let's do some exploring in chapters 12–14. John begins in chapters 12 and 13 by showing us evil. He shows us what we might call the "unholy trinity" of the dragon, the beast, and the false prophet. John wants us to see and recognize the evil that plagues this world. But then in 14:1–5 John shifts our gaze to the other side and shows us good. He shows us an army of God standing on Mount Zion with Jesus. John goes on in 14:6–7 with keeping the focus on good as an angel reminds us to "fear God and give him glory." But then in 14:8–11 John shifts back to focusing on evil. In these verses two more angels warn us away from Rome ("Babylon the great") and worship of anything that isn't God.

John isn't done. He concludes chapter 14 by telling us about two future "in-gatherings." In 14:14–16, John focuses on the harvest or salvation of the faithful; it is a good and wonderful event! In

14:17–20, John tells us of the judgment on those opposed to God; it is the final ending of that which is evil.[1]

That is a lot of back and forth—good then evil, good then evil. It does feel like a ping-pong game, as we keep moving between the two.

What John is doing is showing us both the reality of God and evil in this world. Both are real, both seek our attention, and both have to be dealt with. And his not-so-subtle message in all this is—pick a side! Both God and evil are at work: which side are you going to be on?

John knows full well that there is evil in the world. In fact one of the reasons he wrote Revelation was to "reveal" or unmask evil for what it is. The Roman Empire, the ways of the world, are clearly lifted up in Revelation as evil and opposed to God.

John also knows that God is involved in the world. That is the good news, the power, behind the book. Jesus the Lamb has triumphed; the power of God is at work and God will bring about an entire new creation. For now, though, this world of ours is a strange mixture of good and evil. Both are active, and both vie for our loyalty.

John insists that we see this; then he adds a directive: Pick a side. You can't serve both God and evil. We need to pick one or the other.

That sounds simple enough. But the reality is that Christians often think that they can live with one foot in each. We try to compromise the faith with the ways of a sinful world. That was the temptation at Pergamum and Laodicea in chapters 2 and 3 of Revelation; the people identified themselves as Christians, but Roman ways were awfully appealing. This temptation has plagued the church throughout history. Church history bears witness to religious wars, power grabs by Christians, greed and indifference

---

1. I share a fuller examination of 14:14–20 in my book *Come, Lord Jesus*, 101–8. John in these verses refers to two future in-gatherings at the final judgment. The "harvest" by Jesus ("one like a son of man") is an image for the final salvation of God's people, as harvest in biblical imagery is often an image of the salvation of the faithful. The reaping of the grapes is an image of judgment of those opposed to God.

among people of faith. Christians have tried to claim the faith while allowing, or perhaps more accurately, sharing in the sins of the world. In recent history, Christians in Nazi Germany tried to get along with the Nazi regime; Christians in South Africa supported apartheid; Christians in the United States allowed and even supported Jim Crow laws. Today that struggle continues. Christians in our culture are bombarded with materialism, sexualization, bigotry, and greed, to name just a few. It seems only natural to make our peace with the ways of the world. One of my friends likes to say that many Christians want to follow Jesus but to not be too radical about it. We bear the name of Christian but are all too willing to accept and participate in the wrongs of our day.

And John says no. Period. Pick a side! We are for Jesus or we are against Jesus. As Christians we are to first see that evil and God are both active in this world. We need to honestly assess all that goes on. As we differentiate God from evil, we are to choose to align with the work of God. No compromising. As we've said earlier, Christians are to be "distinctively different" from the ways of the world as we again and again pick the ways of Jesus.

C. S. Lewis has a famous quote that I believe John would love. Lewis wrote, "There is no neutral ground in the universe. Every square inch, every split second, is claimed by God and counterclaimed by Satan." C. S. Lewis saw human life as a continual struggle between God and evil, with Christians called to direct themselves to God again and again and again. John raises the same point in Revelation. The fact is evil is much too active and seductive, too close to each of us, too close to all of our institutions and human affairs. We are called to recognize evil for what it is and then leave it behind as we follow the ways of God.

I began this section with the illustration of a ping-pong game as John shifts our attention back and forth between good and evil. I think there is a point where my illustration breaks down. In a ping-pong game, it is quite obvious which side of the table you are on. When it comes to real life, it isn't so obvious. Good and evil can be hard to differentiate in our actual lives. Satan is a master of deception, and he is skilled at blurring that line between good and evil. In fact in Revelation John astutely notes that evil often disguises itself as good. Evil bills itself as helpful, alluring, as the way to get ahead. Evil can be oh-so-subtle, and we are blind to how we get caught up in the ways of this world.

I remember one of the congregations that I served as pastor. It was a smaller congregation, but we began to grow. New people began coming; they were exploring and growing in the faith and they joined the congregation. The congregation began changing. We were running out of room for Sunday School, we needed to add a second worship service, and new folks were filling old committee positions. Some of the long-time members of the congregation began to object. They didn't want their church to change. They wanted a congregation where they knew everybody and where, I might add, they were in charge. They didn't like some of the new directions and ideas. The growth of the congregation was upsetting to them, and they objected. We ended up taking a year for prayer and Bible study to come to terms with the fact that Jesus always calls for his church to grow.

My longtime members in that congregation didn't see themselves as evil. I believe they were good-hearted people. They just wanted to preserve the congregation they were comfortable with and that they had always liked. That seemed to them a good goal. But in doing so they were moving toward the evil of restricting the growth of Christ's church. We had to work hard to clearly understand what Jesus' goals are for the church. To their credit, as those longtime members more clearly saw the goals of Jesus, they did pick the side of our Lord.

That is part of the trouble with evil. It is so often subtle, comfortable, disguised as good, and looking part and parcel of the ways of this world. We don't see evil for what it is and we end up moving from the ways of the very Savior we confess.

That brings us back to Rev 12–14. John in these chapters is calling for us to clearly differentiate between the ways of the world and the ways of God. John clearly puts evil on one side and God on the other and he calls for us to be carefully discerning. Then he reminds us to pick the side of God in all that we do.

To go a bit further, this is why it is so vital for Christians to constantly focus on Jesus. It is too easy to be distracted, compromised, misled. We must look to Jesus again and again. We must let Jesus continually guide how we see and live our lives. We are to be a people who continually root themselves in the word of God. We are to be a people who use all the spiritual resources that God gives—reading the Bible, worship, the sacraments, prayer, fellowship with other Christians—that we might clearly see the ways of God. We continually look to Jesus and let Him focus our lives.

Good and evil: Both are at work in this world. John assures us that the day will come when evil is banished—that victory has been guaranteed through the cross of Jesus. For now we need to be discerning. We need to focus and choose the side of Jesus no matter what.

Pick a side. It is clear advice and vital advice. May we live always for Jesus Christ.

QUESTIONS

1. Would you say the world is good or bad, or perhaps a strange mixture of both?
2. Name some places where you see evil at work in the world.
3. Name some places where you see God at work in the world.
4. Share examples of where you have seen evil try to make itself look good.
5. What might "picking the side of Jesus" look like in our daily lives?
6. How might we as Christians be "distinctively different" from the world? Share some examples.

Section 15

Come Out of Her!
Revelation 18 for Yesterday, Today, and Tomorrow

ONE OF THE THINGS that I'm learning about the book of Revelation is that it speaks a powerful word to our modern day. Now that shouldn't surprise me. God's Word has a knack for speaking to our present circumstances. But too often when we talk about Revelation, we don't acknowledge that. We have a tendency to read Revelation in one of two ways, and neither is adequate. One way is to read Revelation as an ancient history book. It is seen as a two-thousand-year-old record of concerns that ancient believers had with the Roman Empire, and we leave Revelation in the past. The second way of reading Revelation is to see it in terms of wild futuristic scenarios. We think that Revelation is a book that predicts future tribulations and raptures and battle plans for Armageddon. We look to Revelation for a road map to the future. Neither of those approaches accurately reflect what the book is about nor proclaim the power of the book. The book of Revelation is much, much deeper than either of these approaches indicate.

As I've been doing, I'm going to suggest a different approach to Revelation—that is, to read it in terms of past, present, and future. We begin by reading Revelation in its historical context. Revelation is a historical document, and we need to start there. Revelation was originally addressed to seven specific congregations in ancient Asia Minor, and we need to understand that context. But we don't stop there. After we ask what Revelation said in its original historical situation, we need to move on and ask, What does Revelation say to us in our day? Then we even go one step further and ask, How does Revelation direct us into God's future? The power of God's word is that it is a word that was spoken in the past, continues to speak in the present, and will lead us right into eternity. We need to see all of that as we deal with Revelation and in fact as we read the entire Bible.

For a case in point for all of this, let's look at Rev 18. Revelation 18 is a great example of this. It is a highly stylized, symbolic, artistic piece of literature, and it speaks a powerful word to Christians of all generations. (Let me also acknowledge that I'm in debt for many of these ideas that follow to a book entitled *Revelation* by M. Eugene Boring.)[1]

Revelation 18 is about the destruction of Rome. (Rev 18 uses the word "Babylon," but any good Christian or Jew in the first century would have immediately known that John was speaking of Rome.) Revelation 18 proclaims that the Roman Empire will fall. Rome, the persecutor of the church and the source of so much arrogance and greed, will fall. Revelation 18 is one of the most artistically written passages in the book. The actual fall of Rome is not depicted. John instead writes about how the kings of the earth and the merchants and seafarers mourn the loss of Rome. The readers of Revelation, including us, experience the destruction of Rome through the eyes of Rome's allies and profiteers. Revelation 18 is basically a funeral dirge for Rome and its might.

In the midst of Rev 18, John also instructs the Christians to do two things. First, come out of her. In v. 4 John writes, "Come out of her, my people, so that you do not take part in her sins." Now John isn't telling the Christians to physically move out of the city. The people that John is addressing in his letter already live in Asia Minor; they aren't anywhere near Rome. John is saying keep your distance from Roman values. The Roman Empire has become a place of greed and violence and debauchery and

---

1. Boring, *Revelation*, 188–89.

arrogance. Christians must not make their peace with such things. Move away from such values, John writes, for they lead only to destruction. Live rather with the values given in Jesus Christ. The values at work in the Roman Empire are not acceptable for people of faith. Don't get caught up in them.

And second, John says to rejoice: "Rejoice over her, O heaven, you saints and apostles and prophets!" (v. 20). Now that may sound like strange advice in the midst of a word of destruction. But Christians know that life is always given in Jesus Christ. Jesus is always at work making things new. Even in the midst of hurtful, confusing, and destructive times, Christians dare to be a people of hope and promise. Christians dare to rejoice, even in trying times, because we look to the future with hope. We know that the future is ultimately God's future. This world is redeemed through the cross and carried in the hands of the risen Savior. Christians are to be a people who dare to sing the Lord's song even in midst of trying times.

That was the message of Rev 18 to John's first readers. Now let's jump forward two-thousand years and ask, does this have anything to say to our modern day? We certainly don't live in a time when the Roman Empire is being judged. We pray that we don't endure a time of destruction. Does Rev 18 say anything to us?

I believe it does. In fact it shares a powerful message. We in our modern day live in incredibly trying times. We live in hurtful times, confusing times. Our country is racked with disagreement and anger. We don't trust each other, we don't trust the news we hear, we see the worst in the motives of others, and we too often can't figure out how to even talk about differences. It is a time of division and anger like we have not seen before.

It is precisely here that Rev 18 has a message for us. First, come out of her, my people. In other words, Christians, don't live in the hatred and anger that is becoming all too acceptable. Don't accept the perversions and inflammations that are becoming so common in our day. Leave those things behind, for we as Christians always live with the values given in Jesus Christ. Just as Revelation's first readers were called to leave behind the values of ancient Rome, we are called to leave behind the hatreds and angers that are becoming all too acceptable in our culture. In a time of distrust and despair we dare to be a people who listen to our neighbor, who care for our neighbor, who reach out to all people. We are to be a people of grace and dignity. We intentionally leave behind the divisions of our present day and live in the values of Jesus Christ.

Second, rejoice. Rejoice, because Jesus is Lord and we dare to believe that He is working out his promises for us. Yes, our day struggles and hurts, and we grieve for that. But Christ is bringing in a whole new day. That day has already dawned in an empty tomb. We find our confidence in that. We are a people who sing the Lord's song of hope and newness. That is a song our day needs desperately to hear! We will celebrate and proclaim the victory of Jesus Christ, no matter how dark the world gets, and we will do so right into eternity.

What a word for our day! That's the power of the biblical word. These old, old words break into our present with insight and newness. They shape us now as the people of God; they allow us to encounter the living Lord who gives life to this world and to us. Even more, what a promise for the future! These words give direction and meaning for the future and lead us onward in faith.

What a word in Rev 18! As John wrote—"Come out of her, my people." Christians of all times and places are called to leave behind the world's values of sin and greed—and rejoice in Jesus! Christians of all times and places are called to be people of celebration, worship, and hope in a world that knows too little of hope. May God's word guide us always in Jesus Christ!

That is Rev 18 and that is the book of Revelation. It is an ancient book, of course. It is also a word that speaks to us today, a word of hope and victory. And it is a word that will shape and guide God's people right up to Christ's return!

QUESTIONS

1. We've talked about different ways of reading Revelation. Some people read it only as an ancient history book. Others read it

in a futuristic way, as laying out a road map to the future. We are suggesting a different approach, that we read Revelation in terms of past, present, and future. We begin by asking what Revelation said to its original, past audience. Then from there we ask what it says to us and how it shapes the future. Do you find this to be a helpful approach to Revelation?

2. Are there values and activities in our modern day that Christians need to "come out of"? Name some.

3. How do we rejoice in Jesus as we live in a culture that seems to pay less and less attention to Jesus?

4. How might we as Christians help shape our culture in more godly and positive ways?

5. How does the church be a place of hope in a hopeless world?

Section 16

Armageddon

THERE IS A WORD in the book of Revelation that has captured the modern mind. It is the word "Armageddon." Even people who know little about Revelation know to be nervous about Armageddon. The word has been used in the title of numerous movies and books, and it has been the theme of numerous movies and books. We know to be wary of this great upcoming battle of Armageddon.

In our modern vocabulary, Armageddon has come to refer to the great cataclysmic battle at the end of the world. We expect a battle of nuclear destruction and desolation, a battle that involves armies and weapons from all over the earth. Armageddon has become a way of speaking of total annihilation.

A good question for Christians to ask is, What does Revelation actually say about Armageddon? I think most of us are surprised when we learn what the good Lord actually wants to tell us.

So, let's do a little digging and see what the last book of the Bible says about Armageddon. By the way, Revelation is the only book in the Bible to use this term. Let's see what Revelation intends us to know.

Armageddon is referred to twice in Revelation, in chapters 16 and 19. John likes to introduce important concepts early and then develop them later in the book. That is the case with Armageddon.

ARMAGEDDON

It is introduced in chapter 16 but will only be developed in chapter 19. Here is how the word is introduced in 16:12–16:

> The sixth angel poured his bowl on the great river Euphrates, and its water was dried up in order to prepare the way for the kings from the east. And I saw three foul spirits like frogs coming from the mouth of the dragon, from the mouth of the beast, and from the mouth of the false prophet. These are demonic spirits, performing signs, who go abroad to the kings of the whole world, to assemble them for battle on the great day of God the Almighty. ("See, I am coming like a thief! Blessed is the one who stays awake and is clothed, not going about naked and exposed to shame.") And they assembled them at the place that in Hebrew is called Harmagedon.

Just a bit of background for chapter 16: John has been writing in this chapter about upcoming judgment, most of it aimed at the Roman Empire. Using symbolic language, John refers to Rome as "the beast." To John's mind, the beast/Rome has been exploiting and subjugating the people of the world. The beast is evil, and John is clear that it will answer to God. In chapter 16 judgment is proclaimed against the beast (Rome), the dragon (John's way of referring to Satan), and the false prophet. God knows the evil that is being done against his creation, and it will be stopped.

Interestingly, when judgment is announced, John writes that the kings of the earth respond by gathering together for battle against God. This sinful world doesn't want to listen to God; when judgment is proclaimed, the response is to fight. (Think about that for a moment. You would think that a better response to the warning of judgment would be repentance. But sinners too often don't do that!) Evil—namely the dragon/Satan, the beast/Rome, and the false prophet—gather the nations and the forces to fight against God. The reading ends with the ominous note that they assemble at the place called Armageddon. (Just a note of clarification: some scholars and translators prefer "Harmagedon," others prefer "Armageddon."[1] Both translations refer to the same word

---

1. Koester, *Revelation*, 660.

in Revelation. I'm using Armageddon here as that seems to be the more popular reading in our day.)

Armageddon literally means "the mound of Megiddo." Megiddo is a site in Israel people often visit today. It was the site of a number of Old Testament battles; it is a great image for a place of destruction. But there is an oddity in the title. Armageddon means "the mound or hill of Megiddo." If you have been to Israel, you quickly notice that Megiddo is a plain. There is a bit of a pile from ancient ruins that have been destroyed over the centuries, but the area is a plain. There is no mountain.

So why does John refer to the mound of Megiddo? I suspect this is John's way of reminding us that this is symbolic literature, not a literal recounting of what is to come. It would be analogous in our modern day of writing about "the mountains of Omaha." Anyone who has been to Nebraska knows that Omaha is plains. The language would signal to us that the account isn't to be read as a literal account. The language rather tells us that this reading is using symbols to make a point.

John in chapter 16 tells us that the forces of evil gather together at Armageddon to battle against God. But that is all that John tells us in chapter 16. He sets up the battle, but it is not yet fought. The actual battle waits for chapter 19, and there the battle will be engaged. So, let's move to that passage:

> Then I saw heaven opened, and there was a white horse! Its rider is called Faithful and True, and in righteousness he judges and makes war. His eyes are like a flame of fire, and on his head are many diadems; and he has a name inscribed that no one knows but himself. He is clothed in a robe dipped in blood, and his name is called The Word of God. And the armies of heaven, wearing fine linen, white and pure, were following him on white horses. From his mouth comes a sharp sword with which to strike down the nations, and he will rule them with a rod of iron; he will tread the wine press of the fury of the wrath of God the Almighty. On his robe and on his thigh he has a name inscribed, "King of kings and Lord of lords."

> Then I saw an angel standing in the sun, and with a loud voice he called to all the birds that fly in midheaven, "Come, gather for the great supper of God, to eat the flesh of kings, the flesh of captains, the flesh of the mighty, the flesh of horses and their riders—flesh of all, both free and slave, both small and great." Then I saw the beast and the kings of the earth with their armies gathered to make war against the rider on the horse and against his army. And the beast was captured, and with it the false prophet who had performed in its presence the signs by which he deceived those who had received the mark of the beast and those who worshipped its image. These two were thrown alive into the lake of fire that burns with sulfur. And the rest were killed by the sword of the rider on the horse, the sword that came from his mouth; and all the birds were gorged with their flesh. (19:11–21)

In 19:11 Jesus appears. John writes that a rider comes on a white horse, and John's description makes clear that this is Jesus—"Faithful and True, in righteousness he judges, the Word of God." Jesus is leading the armies of heaven and He has come to reclaim his creation. Jesus is described in magnificent terms as the coming, conquering warrior.

But a little digging is in order here also. In v. 13, it is noted that Jesus' robe is covered in blood. An important question to ask is, Whose blood is it? The first-century Jewish people looked for a messiah who would come and slay Israel's enemies. The blood of those opposed to God would be shed. That isn't what Jesus does. I would suggest that the blood on Jesus' robe is his own! It is his blood, shed on the cross! The incredible message of Revelation, and of the entire New Testament, is that Jesus does conquer. He does so not by destroying his enemies but by dying for the sake of his enemies! It is the crucified One who brings in the kingdom of God!

In chapter 19 Jesus comes, followed by the armies of heaven. In 19:19, John tells us that the beast and the kings of the earth are there with armies to fight against Jesus. We now need to read carefully the description of the battle. What weapons are listed? Is there any mention of nuclear bombs or cruise missiles or tanks?

None that I can find. There is only one weapon that is listed—"from his mouth comes a sharp sword with which to strike down the nations." What is that? The word of God. Revelation previously has described God's word as a sharp two-edged sword. The only weapon that is listed for the battle is the word that comes from Jesus' mouth. And it really isn't much of a battle. Jesus' word immediately overcomes the opposition. In other words, Jesus comes, speaks God's word, and evil is defeated. Period. No lengthy battle or military campaign. Jesus as the word of God simply and totally overcomes evil.

Notice what is going on here. This isn't a prediction of future annihilation. It is a promise of Jesus' triumph. The point here is that Jesus as the word of God overcomes all evil. The ultimate word in the history of this world will be Christ's word of victory. This isn't a prediction of future battle movements, but a promise of God's triumph in Christ!

That is the point of Armageddon. That is a point, a promise, that we need to hear today! Yes, there are problems and struggles and battles in this world. Yes, evil will often seem insurmountable. But Jesus wins! That is the guarantee of Easter morning. Nothing will stop the victory of the crucified One, and all of history can look forward to Jesus Christ. This passage is meant to be a word of assurance for Christians as we go through our lives in this world.

It amazes me how we treat this message of Armageddon. We take a word of promise in the Bible and turn it into a message of destruction. Let's focus instead on the promise! A good exercise for students of Revelation, and students of the Bible, is to look at what the Bible actually says. In this case it is a tremendous word of hope.

Armageddon: We know the word. Let's be sure we also hear the promise!

QUESTIONS

1. What do you think of when you hear the word Armageddon? Have you heard the word? Does this section change how you think of the word?

2. Why do you think John talks about the "mount of Megiddo" when the area is a plain?

3. Do you agree that the blood on Jesus' robe in chapter 19 of Revelation is Jesus' own blood?

4. Revelation refers many times to the fact that Jesus conquers. How does Jesus conquer?

5. What is the promise of this imagery of Armageddon?

6. Do you think the imagery of Armageddon is threat or promise?

Section 17

The Supper of the Birds

ONE OF THE MOST horrifying images in the book of Revelation is found in 19:17–21. It is the image of birds gorging themselves on the bodies of those who fought against God. It is a gut-wrenching, overwhelming, and frightening image. The "flesh of kings, and captains, and mighty men, and horses and their riders, and the flesh of all men" are devoured by birds after a final battle. In fact the birds are said to gorge themselves on the flesh. It is a fearful image. And then the reading goes so far as to refer to this as "the great supper of God." I'm stunned every time I read it. You have to ask, What in the world is going on here?

Let's begin by looking at the passage:

> Then I saw an angel standing in the sun, and with a loud voice he called to all the birds that fly in midheaven, "Come, gather for the great supper of God, to eat the flesh of kings, the flesh of captains, the flesh of the mighty, the flesh of horses and their riders—flesh of all, both free and slave, both small and great." Then I saw the beast and the kings of the earth with their armies gathered to make war against the rider on the horse and against his army. And the beast was captured, and with it the false prophet who had performed in its presence the signs by which he deceived those who had received the mark of the beast

and those who worshipped its image. These two were thrown alive into the lake of fire that burns with sulfur. And the rest were killed by the sword of the rider on the horse, the sword that came from his mouth; and all the birds were gorged with their flesh.

The battle referred to here is the battle of Armageddon. We focused on Armageddon in the previous section. For this section I'd like to focus on the imagery of the birds eating the flesh of those who are defeated.

Let me begin by pointing out that there is good news here. Even in the harsh images, there is good news and that is that evil is defeated. The beast (John's language for the Roman Empire) and the false prophet (images of forces against God) are defeated. That is good news. But then the reading goes further. It says that those who have aligned themselves with evil are not only destroyed, their flesh is eaten by birds. It is a gruesome and horrid image. It sounds vengeful, overly punitive. It raises all sorts of questions: How could a loving God do this? Is God this vengeful? What in the world do we say about this?

Let's see if we can unpack this image and see what John is saying. First, remember that this is an image, a piece of symbolic literature. John is an artist and he teaches and preaches by using images. Revelation is rich in symbols—Jesus as the Lamb, Rome as the beast, and prayer as incense rising to God, to name just a few. When we encounter symbols in Revelation, we ought not to take the symbol literally. Rather we need to ask, What is being said by the symbol? By way of example, back in chapter 1 of Revelation, Jesus is described as having a two-edged sword in his mouth. Please don't take that symbol literally. Jesus isn't walking around with a dagger hanging between his teeth. Rather recognize that this is a symbol, and the question to ask is, What does the symbol say? In Revelation (and in Isa 49:2 and Heb 4:12) a sword is an image for the word of God. When John says that Jesus has a two-edged sword in his mouth, John is saying that Jesus is the one who most profoundly speaks the word of God. Do you want to hear the word of God? Then listen to what comes from the lips of Jesus! He speaks the word; in fact He is the Word!

The point is, don't take the symbol literally. Rather ask what the symbol is saying. And note please, this is not to say that Revelation is not true. Quite the contrary, when the symbols proclaim that Jesus is the Word of God, that is the deepest truth we know! The symbols are artistic and imaginative ways of sharing the truth of God.

Now, back to the image of the birds gorging themselves on the flesh of people. The question we need to ask is, What does this image say? It says a number of things.

First, it is an assurance that those opposed to God will finally be defeated. In the book of Revelation, evil is given every opportunity to repent. When evil refuses to listen to God, it must be stopped as God reclaims his creation. God is victorious in Jesus Christ and God is reclaiming his cosmos. If evil won't repent, it will be stopped because God's rule will be all in all. The victory of Jesus will not allow for anything less.

This image of the birds eating flesh is part of the announcement that Jesus defeats evil. To push this a bit further, think of how powerful this announcement would have been to some of the original readers of Revelation. Revelation was addressed to congregations that included congregations in Smyrna and Philadelphia. These congregations were undergoing persecution and struggles for the faith. Hearing that evil will finally be overcome would be heard as a word of assurance and deliverance. God does overcome the evils of this world.

We need to be reminded of that same word today. There are struggles for modern-day Christians. There are too many persecutions in our day, even close to home. We Christians face times of despair and questioning. One of the clear messages of Revelation is that God wins the ultimate victory, and we can and should take heart in that. God will totally overcome all evil, and the starkness of this bird imagery reinforces that.

There is a second question to ask of this bird imagery, and that is, How does this image function? What does the reading do? What the reading is doing is speaking a word of warning. The function of this passage is to warn people (including us!) away from allegiance to anything that is not God.

The book of Revelation is a powerful combination of warnings and promise. There are warnings aplenty in Revelation; for those who would ignore or oppose God, Revelation warns of judgment to come. But there are promises in Revelation too—many, many promises. The promises in Revelation proclaim that for those who live in Christ, nothing in all of heaven or earth will ever stop God's love. In fact the warnings and promises function together to drive people to God. That is John's intent in Revelation, to drive people to the God who alone can redeem them and give them life.

This passage of the birds gorging on flesh is a word of warning. It is meant to make us recoil at disobedience to God. The very starkness of the image tells us of the seriousness of the matter. John uses a loud and even horrifying picture to let us know that we must heed this warning.

Let me remind you of an example of warning that I shared back in section 10. I wrote about how I warned my children not to take a canoe too far out on the lake that we live on. Once, my children were out on the lake in the canoe and a storm was coming. I yelled at them in louder and louder ways to get their attention. My warnings became more and more intense as the danger was increasing. I think that is what John is doing here. He is using intense imagery to stress his word of warning. There is evil that must be avoided, and John uses stark imagery to tell us that.

That is how warnings function. Some are louder and more graphic to get our attention. I believe that is how these images of the birds function in Rev 19. God's purpose isn't to destroy us. He is rather warning us to avoid things that will destroy us. He is warning us of the danger of following that which is not of God. We live in a world where too many people don't heed that warning. Revelation 19 is loud as it warns of dangers ahead.

Third, one more point on this imagery of the birds: This imagery of the birds feasting and eating flesh in chapter 19 is to be held in contrast with another image, the image of the marriage supper of the Lamb. Earlier in chapter 19, just before our passage, the victory of Jesus is announced. Jesus defeats evil, and particularly the evil of the Roman Empire. In 19:1 and following the heavens erupt in songs of praise and joy and celebration over that. Life is restored, God is victorious, and God's people share in the celebration. In 19:9 this victory celebration is called the marriage supper of the Lamb. The image is of a great feast of celebrating and joy in the presence of our risen Lord.

John in chapter 19 is not so subtly holding up two meals for us. There will be the marriage supper of the Lamb and the supper of the birds gorging themselves on flesh. What John is asking is, Which one would you like to attend? We will all be at one or the other. Which one will you choose? We can actually be a bit facetious here and ask, Would you like to attend a supper or be a supper? John is saying that Christians need to make a choice between God's way and the world's way, and he is laying out the implications of each way. John won't let us be neutral; we are either on the side of God or the side of evil.

Think of how this message would have sounded in the congregation at Laodicea. One of the original recipients of Revelation was a congregation in the city of Laodicea. Rev 3:14–22 is the message to this congregation. That passage reveals that this is a rich church in a rich town. This congregation is content in its own abilities and power. Jesus had said you can't serve God and wealth, but the folks at Laodicea most likely thought they could manage to do both. They are content in their wealth and abilities and power. They think they can live in their wealth, and they have full confidence in the protection and guidance of Rome. They are content in their worldly ways and content to give lip service to God. And Jesus in Rev 3 tells the congregation in Laodicea that they are lukewarm in faith and Jesus can't stand it. In 3:16 Jesus says He will spit them out of his mouth. The message is that the Christians in Laodicea have to make a choice between the ways of God and the ways of an evil world.

I believe this imagery of the two suppers in chapter 19 does the same thing. John is again telling the Christians, you can't be neutral when it comes to faith. You either serve God or the ways of the world. It is a stark choice but it is a real choice. And to push the choice even further, for those who serve God, there is a marriage supper ahead. For those who don't, we are warned in the graphic imagery of the birds.

It is at this point, I believe, that this imagery becomes incredibly powerful and pertinent to us. Too many people in modern American culture have tried to make their peace with both the ways of the world and the ways of God. We want a faith that is comfortable to us, accommodating to the world, but still gives God lip service. Just like the folks in ancient Laodicea, we want to do both. John, in graphic imagery, tells us that we can't. He sets up a choice for us. We are either for God or against God. John is clarifying for us the seriousness of faith, and he allows no compromise in that.

The supper of the birds: It is quite the image. It horrifies us; it startles us. Perhaps that is the point. If anything—anything—pulls us away from faith in Jesus Christ, we have to leave that behind. The life in Christ is too precious, too eternal, to be compromised with the ways of this world.

QUESTIONS

1. What is your initial reaction when you hear of this image of the supper of the birds?
2. Are these explanations helpful in reading this passage of the birds?
3. How does warning function in Revelation?
4. John in Revelation is warning ancient Christians not to compromise with the ways of a sinful world. Do we live in a time when Christians are tempted to compromise with the ways of the world? Can you share some examples?
5. How can we avoid compromising the faith?
6. We are invited to the marriage supper of the Lamb. How does that image make you feel?

Section 18

The Millennium

OUR NEXT TOPIC IN Revelation is one that has created more controversy and debate than any other in the book. It is the topic of the millennium or the one thousand-year reign. (The word "millennium" comes from two Latin words meaning "one thousand years.") In Rev 20 John writes about believers who reign with Christ for one thousand years. It is a brief passage, and the only place in the Bible where a one thousand-year reign is mentioned. But my goodness have Christians through the centuries argued about this!

Let me begin by sharing the passage—Rev 20:4–6:

> Then I saw thrones, and those seated on them were given authority to judge. I also saw the souls of those who had been beheaded for their testimony to Jesus and for the word of God. They had not worshipped the beast or its image and had not received its mark on their foreheads or their hands. They came to life and reigned with Christ a thousand years. (The rest of the dead did not come to life until the thousand years were ended.) This is the first resurrection. Blessed and holy are those who share in the first resurrection. Over these the second death has no power, but they will be priests of God and of Christ, and they will reign with him a thousand years.

The Millennium

For a quick overview of this, John sees thrones and it looks like the thrones are occupied by "those who had been beheaded for their testimony to Jesus." In the previous paragraph, John writes that Satan has been defeated and locked up for a one thousand-year prison sentence in the bottomless pit. Now in our verses some Christians are resurrected to reign with Jesus for the one thousand years. This is the one thousand years that is referred to as the millennium. After the one thousand years, Satan is released and again comes to deceive and attack the nations and the church. Satan is quickly defeated and then thrown into the lake of fire where he joins his associates the beast and the false prophet for all eternity.

Our question, How do we understand this one thousand-year reign? As I said, there have been, and continue to be, incredible arguments about this. There is a "premillennial" position, a "postmillennial" position, and an "amillennial" position; and I would add, there are lots of arguments between the various positions.

The "premillennial" folks believe that first Jesus comes (hence the language of "pre," or before, the millennium). Jesus comes and vanquishes Satan and then the one thousand-year reign begins. This is a very popular idea in our modern day and has been popularized by the Left Behind series of books and movies.

The postmillennial folks take a different track. They believe that things on this earth get better and better for one thousand years, and after the one thousand years, Jesus returns (hence the language of "post," or after, the millennium). The earth gets better and better, and it all culminates with the return of Jesus. This position is often linked with social gospel movements that emphasize the church being involved in and improving the world.

The amillennial position goes back to St. Augustine in the fourth century and even before that. Amillennialism teaches that the millennial language is not to be seen as an exact period of time but as symbolic language. Some amillennialists hold that this millennial language is a way of speaking of the age of the church that began with the first coming of Jesus. According to this train of thought, we are now in the millennium and have been for two thousand years.

(I have to add a fourth insight, and this comes from Dr. Bruce Metzger, a great twentieth-century biblical scholar. Years ago I attended a seminar led by Dr. Metzger where he laid all this out. He then said, "I'm promillennial. You tell me that Jesus is coming? I'm all for it." It was a bit tongue in cheek, but I loved it!)

Given all of this, the question we have to ask is, What does Rev 20 actually say? Let me suggest some points for us to keep in mind. First, let's remember that when John uses numbers in Revelation, they are symbols. John uses numbers not for statistical details but for symbolic insight. So for example, when John writes in chapter 17 that ten kings will rule for an hour, we ought not to think in terms of sixty minutes, nor ten specific monarchs. In chapter 2 when John warns that Christians will be imprisoned for ten days, I don't think he is saying that the persecutions of Christians will only last for a week and a half. John uses numbers symbolically and that is the case with the millennium.

Second, let's let John guide us in how we understand this passage. Many interpreters of Revelation have chosen to let this passage be the key to the whole book of Revelation. That isn't how John treats it. For John this one thousand-year reign is a brief insight on the way to something even more important—namely, the new Jerusalem. For John the goal of the book is the new Jerusalem, the fullness of God's kingdom that comes in chapters 21 and 22. In those chapters John gives us great details and insight. John's treatment of the millennium is much sparser. It is something that John notes but then moves beyond. Now this is not to say that the millennium passage is unimportant. Of course not, for all biblical passages are important and given by God. But let's allow John to guide us as we journey through Revelation, and that means putting the greater emphasis on the new Jerusalem.

So, with all this said, how do we understand this promise of a millennium? I think this millennium passage is John's way of answering a previous question raised in Revelation. John is a very competent author; he doesn't leave things hanging. Sometimes he doesn't answer questions right when they are raised, but he will return to them. Way back in chapter 6, the fifth seal is opened. With the opening of the fifth seal (6:9–11), there is persecution on the earth. Christians are martyred for their witness to the faith. Their blood is being shed, and they cry out to God, "How long?" (v. 10). It is a powerful cry, a cry asking for justice and asking if God has forgotten them. It is an important question: Lord, your people are suffering. Have you abandoned us?

Note, this question is not answered in chapter 6. The martyrs are rather given a white robe and told to wait as more persecutions happen. It is an ominous warning that more persecutions are coming for God's faithful. The question remains, Is God going to remember his saints? Have the martyrs been abandoned by the very Lord they confessed? The question, a very real question even in our day, just hangs there begging for an answer.

I believe the point of the millennium in chapter 20 is to answer that question. John is a very gifted author; he isn't about to let such an important question go unanswered. And so in chapter 20 with the millennium John is saying, God hasn't forgotten his martyrs. God will never forget his people. God rather has a one thousand-year reign coming for you to share in. The millennium becomes a highly stylized and symbolic vision that proclaims the faithfulness of God. The martyrs who by worldly standards seem lost and forgotten are instead revealed to share in the conquering and rule of Jesus Himself! God does remember his saints! God does deliver his people! With that assurance we can move onward to the new Jerusalem.

I believe the point of this millennium passage is not to try to figure out a divine time line as we seek to get a preview of the plans and timing of God. We are in fact warned against doing that a number of times in Revelation; and whenever people try to do so anyway, it always leads to confusion and misunderstanding. Let's rather appreciate this millennium passage for what it is, a promise, an assurance, that God always remembers his people. We may feel forsaken, but God never loses sight of us. Christians will reign with Christ! We can set our very souls on that promise!

Now as I write this, I realize that my thoughts here are not going to be satisfactory to some readers. We by nature want more answers! We have all sorts of questions as we read this millennium passage: What will reigning with Jesus be like? When will it happen? How does all this work out? I think the best thing to say is, let's follow Revelation closely here. John in chapter 20 doesn't address those questions. Now when we get to the new Jerusalem in chapters 21 and 22, John is going to have all sorts of insights and details to share, and that is going to be great fun. But for now, let's follow John's lead and not let our curiosity get us out ahead of him. Let's see this millennium passage for what it is: a promise that God will take care of his martyrs and his people.

Again, think of how beautiful and necessary this promise is! We, in all our struggles and hurts, will reign with Jesus Christ. Jesus Himself guarantees it. Yes, we will hurt and struggle. Yes, for all of us there can be times when we question and wonder about God. But our Lord never wavers. He will always hold us and care for us and we will share in his victory!

I also think it is vital that we see this promise in its larger dimension of Christian martyrdom. Sometimes we get the idea that persecution and martyrdom is a thing of the past and we don't have to ask painful questions about persecution anymore. We need to be reminded that persecution for the faith has not disappeared, and Revelation warns us that it will not. As I shared in an earlier section, the century that saw the most Christians put to death for the faith is the twentieth century, and the twenty-first century is on pace to set a new record. Persecution is a reality for many of our brothers and sisters across the globe. I also fear, as our own American culture becomes less and less Christian, that more persecution is coming for the faithful in this country. We need to know Jesus' promise that He will never forget or forsake us no matter what we face.

That is exactly what Rev 20:4–6 is about. Of course, explore this passage, pray about it, and let your imaginations be shaped by these powerful symbols. But most of all hear the promise: You, and Christians of all times and places, are safely in the hands of Jesus. We will share in his glorious reign!

The Millennium

QUESTIONS

1. Have you previously heard of the millennium? What have you heard? Are you familiar with any of the approaches that are listed here?

2. Do you remember the questions of the martyrs in chapter 6:9–11? Do you think that this millennium passage answers those questions?

3. What do you think of the idea that this millennium passage is a promise that God will always remember his people?

4. Have you even felt forsaken then realized that you are in the hands of Jesus? What was your experience?

5. Will we share in the reign of Christ? How might you envision that?

Section 19

The Great White Throne

ONE OF THE MOST stunning images in the book of Revelation is that of the great white throne. In 20:11–15 John writes of a throne—a huge, magnificent throne—occupied by God Himself. All human beings stand before the throne to give account of their lives. I have to confess nervousness every time I read this passage.

Let's do some digging into this image. For background, in the previous chapters and verses, John has told us of the final battles against evil. Those battles are now completed. All that is opposed to God's reign has been overcome; Satan and the beast and the false prophet have all been thrown into the lake of fire. Evil is done. In place of the battles a new image appears. John continues in 20:11–12:

> Then I saw a great white throne and the one who sat on it; the earth and the heaven fled from his presence, and no place was found for them. And I saw the dead, great and small, standing before the throne, and books were opened. Also another book was opened, the book of life. And the dead were judged according to their works, as recorded in the books.

Evil is destroyed, and John now sees the Almighty, seated on his throne. The remnants of the earth and sky, the remnants of this broken creation, flee from the sheer grandeur of God. All the dead now stand before the throne as books are opened.

It is an amazing picture. Use your imagination to visualize this in your mind. I imagine a huge, overpowering, fearful, magnificent, glorious throne, now in the very midst of us. It is God, seated on the throne, in all his power and might! As I envision it, I feel a strange combination of awe, fear, wonder, glory, and worry. All people of all time and history, including you and me, stand before the God of all creation. This is an image that has captured imaginations for centuries. And the message is clear. Each one of us will stand before God to give account of our lives.

It is an overwhelming, multi-layered image. For starters, the throne reminds us that the ultimate reality of life is God. Our lives, this creation, began in God and will end in God. We will give account to Him. I am responsible to my creator.

Even more, it is a sobering image. I, in all my brokenness and sin, will stand before God. That worries me. The sad fact of my life is that I don't always prioritize God. I too often don't live as my Savior would have me. When it comes to sin, I'm guilty! This image of standing before the throne causes me to reflect on the shortcomings, the failures, the sins of my life. It forces me to see my own unworthiness and directs me to refocus my life. It raises questions for me: Am I listening to the Lord who is the source and goal of life? Am I really working to follow Him? In all honesty I too often lose sight of Him; I rather get all caught up in myself. I overlook the very Lord in whose presence I live. This image of standing before the throne of God reminds me of how often God is not the focus of my life.

Even more, this image drives me to Jesus. When I think in terms of standing before God, I realize again my need for the Savior. As I stand before God it will be clear that I am a sinner. This image strips away all the pretenses I have and leads me back to my only hope, the cross of Jesus.

I believe John wants us to see all of this in this image. God is the source, the goal, of life. We will stand before Him, and we have not lived as He directs us. But thanks be to God, God has given a Savior who gives new life to sinners like us.

The great white throne: It is a powerful image and one for us to keep in mind for all of life.

With all that said, let me note another point from the reading. Did you notice how the reading stated that books were opened? Verse 12 specifically says books in the plural, and references are made in the whole passage to two sets of books. When we stand before God, it is not one set of books that is opened but two. That is strange. God has more than one set of books? If a human business has more than one set of books, it usually means they are up to something unlawful and trying to hide something corrupt. I'm quite sure that John isn't suggesting that of God. But why two sets of books?

John uses the image of two sets of books to address an age-old dilemma in Christian theology. As Christians rooted in Scripture, we need to say two things that don't always fit together well. First, we are saved solely by grace. We aren't restored to God by the goodness of our deeds; our works don't contribute to our redemption. Our salvation and new life are a gift given us in Jesus Christ. But second, we also want to say that our works matter. What we do with our lives as Christians is important. We are accountable to God to live faithfully. The question becomes, how do you proclaim both of these? How do you say that we are saved by grace and also our works do matter? When you try to say both of these things together, it can get confusing. For example, when you say we are saved by grace, it seems logical to conclude that our works are unimportant. Conversely, when you say that our works are important, it seems logical to conclude that our works must then contribute at least something to our salvation. How do you put all of this together?

In fact, theologians and biblical scholars have argued about how to say both of these for centuries. This is one of the central issues behind Paul's letters to the Corinthians. The Christians in Corinth knew that they were saved by grace. Because of that they concluded that their works didn't matter, and therefore they could do whatever they wanted to, sinful or not. Basically their thought was, Jesus is going to forgive us anyway, it doesn't matter what we do. Paul of course doesn't agree. Paul instead writes, yes, it does matter how you live. One of the key questions behind the letters to the Corinthians is how do you say both that we are saved by grace and our works do matter?

So, given all of that, how do you balance both of these? John has an incredibly insightful solution. John is an artist, so he paints a word picture with two sets of books: "And I saw the dead, great and small, standing before the throne, and books were opened. *Also another book was opened*, the book of life. And the dead were judged according to their works, as recorded in the books" (v. 12, emphasis mine). John distinguishes the book of life from a first set of books. One set is the books of what we have done, our deeds: "And the dead were judged according to their works, as recorded in the books." That reminds us that our works matter and we will account to God for our deeds. But John then distinguishes "the book of life" from this set of books: "Also another book was opened." That is the listing of those saved by grace. It is a reminder that salvation is finally a gift, it is for those whom Jesus has written into "the Lamb's book of life" (21:27).

Which of these sets of books are true? They both are! John doesn't worry about fitting all this together in a neat, logical formula. He rather paints a picture to affirm two truths that he deeply believes. The first is that what we do matters. We are called to live faithfully. Second, just as clearly John adds, we are saved solely by Jesus Christ. Salvation is finally and always a gift. As Christians we need to lift up and live with both of these truths in all their totality and wonder.

The great white throne: It is a powerful image. It is a reminder to focus everything we do on Jesus Christ. He is the Alpha and the Omega, the one to whom all of life is to be directed. We are to be obedient to Him; we will stand before Him. It is also a reminder of the grace of our Lord, the author of the "book of life" that is written preciously for sinners like us!

QUESTIONS

1. In your mind, how do you envision the throne of God?
2. How does it make you feel to know that you will stand before the throne of God?
3. Does this image of the throne serve to drive you to the forgiveness of Christ?
4. What do you think of this image of two sets of books? Do our works matter? Are we saved by grace? How do we hold all of this together?
5. Are you written in "the Lamb's book of life"? How do you know?

Section 20

The New Jerusalem—Part 1

WE HAVE COME TO the new Jerusalem. We've made it to the end of Revelation, chapters 21 and 22. Our journey brings us to the crescendo, the high point of the book. John now gives us a view into the glory of what awaits us in the fullness of God's plan.

In these last two chapters of Revelation John shows us the new heaven and the new earth. John refers to all this as the "new Jerusalem." We would probably call it "heaven" or "eternity." It is our eternal dwelling place, in the glory and love of our eternal God. The view is staggering! John devotes chapters 21 and the opening verses of chapter 22 to this. We will devote two sections to this as well. In this section we will look at what John shares in chapter 21; in the next section we'll look at chapter 22. We won't cover all that is in both chapters; there is too much packed in. I'd suggest reading these chapters for yourselves time and again! I'll lift up for you some of the highlights to help you in your exploration of this.

First a word of clarification: As I mentioned, when we talk about the eternity that awaits us, we usually use the word "heaven." We talk of "going to heaven." We talk of heaven as our eternal abode. John uses different language for this reality. He uses the phrase "the new Jerusalem," and that is significant. First, when we think of heaven in our day, we tend to think in individualistic terms. We see heaven as angels drifting around on clouds, perhaps with harps, all on their own. John says no, eternity will be a city—or better, a community! God's will is that God's people always share in community. That is true for this life now, and it will reach its culmination in the new Jerusalem to come. In the grace of God, we belong together!

In addition, calling eternity "the new Jerusalem" allows John to continue with imagery he has been developing throughout Revelation. Revelation in many ways has been a tale of two cities. There is ancient Rome; there is the new Jerusalem. John has repeatedly asked his readers, do you want to participate in Rome, that drunken whore that is polluting and desecrating the earth? Or do you want to share in the city of God that breaks in from eternity, the new Jerusalem to come? John repeatedly asks us where we want our citizenship.

One more suggestion as we prepare to look at the new Jerusalem: That is, as you read chapters 21 and 22 in Revelation, use your imaginations. In fact, let your imaginations soar! John isn't giving us a literal description of the glory to come. God's glory is beyond human visions and words. Rather John appeals to our imaginations to give us a sense of the pure wonder that God has in store. John is an artist who paints pictures with words to give us a sense of what is finally beyond our senses. Let your imaginations run with these images in chapters 21 and 22.

Let's look at some of what John tells us. First, promises! John writes in 21:3–4:

> See, the home of God is among mortals.
> He will dwell with them;
> they will be his peoples,
> and God himself will be with them;
> he will wipe every tear from their eyes.
> Death will be no more;
> mourning and crying and pain will be no more,
> for the first things have passed away.

These are incredible promises and they just keep coming one after the other! God will dwell with us. You and I, humble sinners

The New Jerusalem—Part 1

that we are, will share in the complete presence, the fullness and joy, of the Almighty. Going further, John writes that God will be our God, and we are his people. In other words, our deepest identity, given and guaranteed in God Himself, is that we are God's own. There is value and worth and dignity for who we are, because it is given in the creator Himself! John then charges on and lists former plagues of human life (death, mourning, crying, and pain) that have now passed away.

Verse 5 continues with all of this and God Himself speaks. He says, "See, I am making all things new." That is my favorite promise in the book! We presently live lives of brokenness and hurt in a world of darkness and despair. But God will—and even more now is—making us and all things new. There is light, there is newness, and there is victory, and nothing will stop it!

Chapter 21 first shares these glorious promises. Second, John tells us about an eternal gift. In both v. 2 and v. 10 John speaks of the "new Jerusalem coming down out of heaven from God." Our English translation makes this sound like a one-time event. Our English reading sounds like at some point in the future God's eternity will overtake the earth. The Greek original is much richer! In the Greek that John uses, there is a verb tense that is hard to translate into English. What John actually writes is that the new Jerusalem will continually come down and transform this creation. The image is of a forever outpouring of God's grace as all things are continually made new. The grace and goodness of God literally envelope and overflow us for all eternity. It is a giving, a victory, that just won't stop.

Third, John shares some mind-blowing details about the new Jerusalem! In verse 15 he tells us that the holy city is "foursquare" or a cube. How can a city be a cube? It is geometrically and architecturally impossible. But John isn't writing about architecture, he is proclaiming good news. A cube in the ancient world was a symbol of perfection; the new Jerusalem will be perfect. Moreover, in the Old Testament temple, the holy of holies, the place of God's presence, was described as a cube. John is saying that the entire city of new Jerusalem will now be the place of God's presence. We will be totally in the grace of God.

Another detail: in v. 12 John says that there will be twelve gates to the city, and each gate will be a pearl. (It is from this that we get the image of the "pearly gates." But in our contemporary conversations we talk about one set of gates, usually guarded by St. Peter. John envisions twelve gates, always open, guaranteeing access.) John says these gates of heaven will be pearls. Think about that for a moment. How would a pearl function as a gate? But again, that isn't the point. The point is glory and wonder.

In vv. 18 and 21 John goes on and writes that the city and street is made of pure gold, transparent as glass. I've never seen gold so pure it is transparent. But again, that's not the point. The point is the glory and wonder that awaits.

In v. 22 John says there is no need for a temple. John is borrowing a lot of this imagery from the Old Testament book of Ezekiel. Ezekiel had a vision of a restored Jerusalem, and in the restored city is a temple. But for John, the new Jerusalem doesn't need a temple. In Ezekiel, the temple is the place of God's presence. But for John, the new Jerusalem doesn't need a temple because God's presence fills the entire city. And to push further in v. 23, there is no sun or moon for the glory of God is its light and that fills the city.

One more detail that is too often overlooked, but John repeats it twice. In v. 24 John writes, "The kings of the earth will bring their glory into it." In v. 26 John repeats and expands, "People will bring into it the glory and the honor of the nations." If I'm reading this correctly, John is saying that what is good in this creation will be brought into the new Jerusalem to come. In other words, John isn't against creation or human achievement. John recognizes that there is good in that which is done on this earth; in fact that which is good and honorable on this earth will be taken into the new Jerusalem. What a statement of God's respect for us! The good we create and do in this lifetime will be carried with us into the new life to come! And I might add, that insight always gives me pause. I have to ask myself, what in my life am I doing that will be carried

The New Jerusalem — Part 1

into the new Jerusalem? I'm quite sure it isn't my ownership of my house or car or my bank account. What will I carry into the new Jerusalem? Perhaps the relationships I have formed, the decency I can show others, and the goodness I can develop. I believe those things will come with us into the new Jerusalem. It is a powerful reminder to focus our lives on what truly matters.

One of the joyful exercises in reading Revelation is to simply unpack these images in Rev 21 and 22. The gifts, the wonder, just keep coming and coming. To go a bit further, I have been saying all along that Revelation is a book of promise. Nowhere is that clearer than in these last chapters. Let your imaginations and your hearts soar as you envision the wonder that God has prepared for you, for me, and for all his people.

QUESTIONS

1. What is your vision of heaven? What do you think it will be like?
2. What do you think of John's vision of the new Jerusalem? Does anything in particular excite you?
3. God promises to make all things new. What "newness" do you look forward to?
4. Chapter 21 shares many "details" or images of the new Jerusalem. Which detail is the most significant for you?
5. What do you look forward to in the eternity, the new Jerusalem, to come?
6. What in your life do you think you will carry with you into the new Jerusalem?

Section 21

The New Jerusalem—Part 2

IN CHAPTER 22 JOHN continues with the tour of the new Jerusalem: more visions of glory and goodness; and more visions that overwhelm our senses and give us a glimpse into the wonder that God prepares for eternity. It is interesting to me that most of the images in this opening section of chapter 22 are taken from two Old Testament sources, the book of Genesis with the garden of Eden story and the book of Ezekiel with Ezekiel's vision of the city/temple restored. As John looks to God's future, he deliberately draws from the biblical past.

Let's look in detail at 22:1–5. What John writes here is so powerful that I think the best approach is to simply share the passage with you, and then highlight what John has written.

> Then the angel showed me the river of the water of life, bright as crystal, flowing from the throne of God and of the Lamb through the middle of the street of the city. On either side of the river is the tree of life with its twelve kinds of fruit, producing its fruit each month; and the leaves of the tree are for the healing of the nations. Nothing accursed will be found there any more. But the throne of God and of the Lamb will be in it, and his servants will worship him; they will see his face, and his name will be on their foreheads. And there will be no more night; they

The New Jerusalem—Part 2

need no light of lamp or sun, for the Lord God will be their light, and they will reign forever and ever.

John now introduces us to "the river of the water of life," which flows from God's throne right through the middle of the city. Let your imaginations go to work with this image. In my mind I see a beautiful, bright, crystal-clear river rushing forth from God's throne. It is life, abundant life, literally cascading from God. This water/life cascades over rocks, shimmering and bouncing and splashing in the light. There are rainbows and prisms formed above the bright water, and the water is so clear you can see everything in it. The water splashes over us, giving life to each of us and to the entire city. It is an ever-flowing river as God's gift of life just keeps pouring out forever and ever. What a glorious image of God's life given for God's people.

Often when I teach a class on Revelation and get to this point, I'm tempted to make the class stop and sing "Shall We Gather at the River." The song is based on this passage and captures it well. I love to study Revelation, but I also want to sing it and proclaim it in worship. Revelation and its images are just so, so rich, and some of that richness can only be experienced in worship!

John continues with more images. On either side of the river is the tree of life. This tree produces twelve different kinds of fruit, one kind for each month. Once again, John is taking our imaginations and stretching them to the breaking point. How can one tree be on two sides of a river? How can one tree produce twelve different kinds of fruit? Agriculture just doesn't work this way. But again, John isn't writing about farming. He is telling us of, showing us, the sheer abundance of God. Food, water, love—all are in abundance and cascading down all around us.

Perhaps there is an echo here of an Old Testament promise. In the Old Testament there was an expectation that in the messianic age to come, there would be an abundance of food and wine. A tree producing twelve types of fruit echoes that abundance.

Even more significant, note the image of the tree of life. In a few simple words John has captured the biblical journey. Way back in Genesis, in the opening pages of the Bible, God put Adam and Eve in the garden of Eden. The tree of life was in the midst of the garden. But Adam and Eve sin, they fall from God, and they are removed from the garden. They are separated from the tree of life, or maybe better, life itself. Humans have become beings unto death, with each life limited and ended by the age-old destroyer.

The Bible has been the story of God's work to deliver us from death. From early Genesis through the Exodus though the history of Israel through the prophets, God has been at work. That work reaches its crescendo in Jesus Christ as Jesus suffers, dies, and rises from the dead; it continues as the apostles spread the word. Death is overcome! We are invited back to God, the source of life. Now, on the last page of the Bible, the journey is complete. We again stand before the tree of life. We again share in the wonder, the life, the fullness of God. And now nothing will change that. That is the promise for eternity!

Let me move on to the next line of chapter 22, a line which I confess has become more and more precious to me. John continues, "The leaves of the tree are for the healing of the nations." Let that sink in. God is going to heal the nations. Come, Lord Jesus, and do it! We live in a world of hatred and destruction and war—of distrust, chaos, and annihilation. We can't stop the madness; each war is inevitably followed by another. I watch the evening news and I want to scream. John reminds us in a picturesque and powerful promise that God will do what we can't. God will heal the nations! We dare to look forward to—we dare to proclaim and live for—peace and newness. God will heal the nations.

John continues by reminding us that nothing accursed will be in the new Jerusalem. All that is evil and destructive is left behind. The throne of God and the Lamb are the center, and we, God's servants, will worship Him.

John then moves on even more powerfully. In vv. 3–5 John is writing about the "servants of God" and refers to the servants as "they." I would suggest instead of "they" we could read "we," because we are included in this group. We, and all the servants of God, will see the face of God and God's name will be on our foreheads. The name of God on the forehead is a reference to the old Jewish practice of the high priest once a year entering the holy of holies in the Jerusalem temple. The holy of holies was the place where God's immediate presence was; only the high priest could enter there and then only once a year. The priest would do so with the name of God written on his forehead. Now, John promises, we will all be in the immediate presence of God, and John underscores that by saying that we will carry God's name on our foreheads. Moreover, John shares, we will see God's face. That sounds powerful, overwhelming. What could that mean?

Richard Bauckam, in his book *The Theology of the Book of Revelation*, shares a most helpful insight. Bauckam writes, "The face expresses who a person is. To see God's face will be to know who God is in his personal being."[1] It will be to know God, to experience God, to be overwhelmed by the glory and love of God. It will be to know the full immediacy of our creator. There can be nothing more precious!

John continues on in v. 5, and he shifts his metaphor to light, God's own light. John reminds us in the new Jerusalem night will be no more and there will be no need of lamps, for God Himself will be the light. It is as the Gospel of John promised: the light has completely taken over the darkness. We are in the total abundance of God.

John concludes this vision by sharing that we will reign with God forever and ever. I have to note, for many years I saw this as confusing. My question was, Who will we reign over? Reigning to my mind means power over others, but now in the new Jerusalem, who is there for us to reign over?

I've come to realize that my question totally missed the point of what John is saying. Richard Bauckham again has a helpful insight here. John's comment is meant to remind us that God's kingdom is quite unlike the rule of Rome. In the Roman Empire, and I'd add all other empires that have existed since the time of John, to reign meant to have power over people. Our concepts of kingdom involve domination and force—that is, to be over other people. God in his eternal kingdom redefines that. In God's grace,

---

1. Bauckham, *Theology of Revelation*, 142.

reigning is to be shared. God doesn't dominate us; He shares life with us. Rather than defend his throne, He invites us to share his throne. The kingdom that is coming is about sharing and giving and empowering. That is what we will share in for all eternity.[2]

What a crescendo for the book of Revelation! What a vision, what promises! Water of life, abundance of fruit, leaves of healing, seeing the face of God, living in the light of God, reigning with God—all of this is promised for you and me. That's the point. God is indeed making all things new!

QUESTIONS

1. Out of all these images in chapter 22, which is your favorite? Why?
2. What do you think it might mean to reign with God forever and ever?
3. How do you envision the "river of the water of life"? What does this image say to you?
4. The Bible begins in Genesis and ends in Revelation with the tree of life. What does that image say to you?
5. What do you think of the promise that God will heal the nations?
6. How might these promises shape how you live now?
7. What might it mean for you to see the face of God?

---

2. Bauckham, *Theology of Revelation*, 142.

Bibliography

Bauckham, Richard. *The Theology of the Book of Revelation.* New Testament Theology. Cambridge: Cambridge University Press, 1993.
Boring, M. Eugene. *Revelation.* Interpretation. Louisville: John Knox Westminster, 1989.
Braaten, Mark. *Come, Lord Jesus: A Study of Revelation.* 2007. Reprint, Collegeville, MN: Liturgical Press, 2018.
Caird, G. B. *The Revelation of Saint John.* Black's New Testament Commentary. Peabody, MA: Hendrickson, 1966.
Collins, Adela Yarbro. *Crisis and Catharsis: The Power of the Apocalypse.* Philadelphia: Westminster, 1984.
Forde, Gerhard. *Where God Meets Man: Luther's Down-to-Earth Approach to the Gospel.* Minneapolis, MN: Augsburg, 1972.
Johnson, Darrell W. *Discipleship on the Edge: An Expository Journey through the Book of Revelation.* Vancouver, BC: Regent College, 2004.
Koester, Craig R. *Revelation.* Edited by John Collins. The Yale Anchor Bible. New Haven: Yale Univeresity Press, 2014.
———. *Revelation and the End of All Things.* Grand Rapids: Eerdmans, 2001.
Metzger, Bruce. *Breaking the Code Understanding the Book of Revelation.* Nashville: Abingdon Press, 1993.
Rossing, Barbara. *The Rapture Exposed: The Message of Hope in the Book of Revelation.* Boulder, CO: Westview, 2004.
Svanoe, Rolf D. *The Beast in the Pulpit, the Lamb in Our Hearts: Preaching the Book of Revelation in Mainline Churches Today.* Lima, OH: CSS, 2021.
Tertullian. *Apology.* In *The Ante-Nicene Fathers*, edited by Philip Schaff and Allan Menzies, 3:107–108. 10 vols. Grand Rapids: Christian Classics Ethereal Library, 1885.

www.ingramcontent.com/pod-product-compliance
Lightning Source LLC
Chambersburg PA
CBHW050835160426
43192CB00010B/2039